You told me once
  that you cared about me
in this dawn of a new year
I wonder if it might not be an end
  to the night of madness
A dawn of hope
   where the mistakes of yesterday
    can be forgotten
in hopes of starting anew
    without yesterday's crimes

The Forestal
Copyright © 2014 by Blaze Ward
Published by Knotted Road Press
www.KnottedRoadPress.com

ISBN: 978-1499260328

Cover and interior design copyright © 2014 by Knotted Road Press
www.KnottedRoadPress.com

This book is licensed for your personal enjoyment only. All rights reserved. This is a work of fiction. All characters and events portrayed in this book are fictional, and any resemblance to real people or incidents is purely coincidental. This book, or parts thereof, may not be reproduced in any form without permission.

The Forestal
Blaze Ward

Knotted Road Press
www.KnottedRoadPress.com

Also By Blaze Ward

Beyond the Mirror: Fantastic Worlds

Stories
Approacheth the Wyvern
Death Key for the Great Khan
Meat Shield
The Desert Ring
The Mirror
The Popcorn Kitten
The Slave Market

The Forestal
Blaze Ward

Table of Contents

Orgins: Seeker's Tale
    The Dawn of Hope   3
    Dawnsquest   19
    Starfall   35

Travels: The Winterstone Chronicles
    the Winterstone Chronicles   55
    the Blacksmith's Song   69
    Emerald   83

Outcomes: The War Of The Dragons
    Dragonquest   107
    Dragon   121
    The Forestal   129
    the Great Wyrm   139
    Tapestry   153

Origins: Seeker's Tale

The Dawn of Hope

Chapter 1: Outcast

So many times I wanted to call you up
to apologize for everything
  but there was always something else
    to add
      to the list of sins

One morning it was simply too much
I could no longer bear the weight
  of the world
  on my shoulders
    when I had done so little

One mistake became ten thousand
but when I sought to cry out
  to end the farce
it became ten million

the only recourse left me
  was to climb the highest mountain
where you could not follow
  and there find a kind of escape
where the sins of mankind
  were not mine alone to suffer for

You told me once
  that you cared about me
in this dawn of a new year
I wonder if it might not be an end
  to the night of madness
A dawn of hope
   where the mistakes of yesterday
    can be forgotten
in hopes of starting anew
   without yesterday's crimes

I had climbed the mountain in desperation
but looking back I see no path up
so I think I am safe here
  where no one can follow

If we cannot end
  this night of madness
I shall leave to make my own dawn
and forget you
  to your high tower
   and your troll
for I see the old desert
  suddenly stretched out before me
It is
  my own dawn of hope
beginning

Chapter 2: Memories of the Oasis

High strong gray walls
   to keep the world at bay
  palm trees and a pool of water
  a world removed from the desert without
   safe and cool and quiet

The stone surrounding is generations old
   scarred by fire and storm and flood
 In the oasis I healed my poisoned soul
   safe from the brutalities of memory

When you first appeared
   I saw the hunger in your soul
    for the shade and sweet water
   so I opened the gates
I had forgotten
   how much poison a soul could suffer
   and still survive
until I saw you standing there
   shivering with the desert fever

When you needed the solitude
   I left the ramparts for the sand
   and we talked but rarely
   when the winds brought me near

Once I even returned
   for a few brief moments
   before the dawn cast us apart

I remember from the old days
   the moonlight in your eyes
   like a flash of brilliant silver in the dark
But yesterday I saw the sunlight break out
   for just a moment of time
   until you blinked
   maybe I imagined it all

Origins: Seeker's Tale

Do you remember the sound of the winds?
   blowing outside the ramparts
   an eerie keening on the rocks
Once it inspired a symphony in your name
   written by the guardian of these walls
   do you remember Blaze?

I remember his song
   endless like the grand epics
   a mountain tall and a continent wide
   a monument to the two children we once were

But there was never an ending to the verse
   and even now I can only write a movement
   only find a distant hill to watch
   only remember the oasis
  and you

Chapter 3: Dawnsquest

Silverfire shatters the darkness before me
   exploding into the brilliance of morning
   as night flees westward behind
   and I flee into the rising sun

It is dawn
   where auguries once bespoke Night Eternal
   enfolding daylight's promise
But the Master of Darkness failed

Where once he tried to claim all
   he now stands banished
   by the dawn of hope

Morningfire paints the horizon silver
  and smiles at me
   with warm allure
    off the midnight frost
There is now ice and fire
   where once ice ruled alone
Frost fails
   as dark once did
   and warmth returns as well

I wonder if the world remembers
   what the day was
before the dark took us all
   in his cold quiet shadows

And so it begins
   lighting up the road I remember
   giving me the Dawn's quest
   the dream I had lost in battle

In the first kiss of daylight
   it all comes back to me

The good and the evil
   the night and the day
  the anger and the sorrow
for dawnsquest is also goodbye

Already I feel the day race by
the Master of Darkness laughs
It is winter yet in this world
  and his nights are longer than my days
He laughs and the world weeps
  reminded of sadness unbanished
  but it is the Dawn of Hope

Chapter 4: Lost

If I closed my eyes
   for a moment
would I lose you?

Would darkness overtake us
   in the hollow shell
   of a quiet eternity?
Would it swallow our steps
   leaving only the memory
   of saying goodbye?

Could we ever come back
   to the dawn we knew
   when the world was young
   and dreams stretched out forever?
Or have we finally lost the way
   lost the passion
   lost...
      ...the dream?

I still seek that yesterday
   the carefree boy
   the troubled lass
  a moment of purity
  one last taste of innocence

They're all still out there
somewhere
 in the darkness
   a candle
    and a prayer

By moonlight
   the fire in your eyes
   touches me once more
Lovers once, and again
Lost before; between; beyond

When I sleep
   I hear your last words
   and taste that one last tear
   as the cloak of darkness
embraces me

 like fog it came
I lost my road
 and never made it back
   from where I went astray

Chapter 5: The Citadel

Can you feel the sands burn
  in the noontime sun?
  or see the rising storm
    where the dunes meet the sky?

My path brings me here
  the wastes beyond the world
  the dune-sea graveyard
    where fools and kings reside

The first step into the desert
  back from the world beyond
  is a nightmare I know all too well
    from countless dreams

Can you hear the wind keening?
  a deathsong on the rocks
    haunting me with dreams and memories
Yesterday's failures
  loom giant before me
Faces etched into a mountainside
  mocking me

There is a handprint
  on the stone before me
    and suddenly I realize
  that my steps have brought me back
to the ruins of the Citadel
  a broken wall around the oasis
    like I first found it years ago

Inside, at my feet
  a pile of crystal shards
    once upon a time
  that was my heart
Yesterday's broken dream

Origins: Seeker's Tale

Around me
  I feel the presence of the Guardian
  a ghost still haunting these ruins
    keeping wild dogs and storm's fury at bay

I find the pool
  still ringed by the palms I knew
  the sands still cool
    in the noonday heat
  the water still pure and sweet

I would have sworn
  that the storms had reclaimed it all by now
    burying it like my memories
    erasing the spot in the desert
  where I learned to survive

But perhaps
  like my memories
  the winds have uncovered it again
    for me to find

It has barely changed
  for all that the sands have blown
    all that I have traveled
    and all that I have lost
  in the years between

In the harsh noontime sun
  and long years of wind
    no other tracks mar the sand
  and even mine are slowly blowing away

I fear just a little
  that yesterday's monument
    is tomorrow's altar
  that memories and dreams
    somehow survived the chaos
      of the storm's fury

But it is here
  that the dawnsquest brings me
  to hear the Guardian's song
    still echoing off the rocks
  though we both passed to the sands
    long ago

In the shadows I hear him keen
  and for just a moment
  I join him
Mourning all we lost
  from the days
    when we stood on the walls
  together
Invincible

Chapter 6: Returned

In my heart
   I always feared
     a return to the sands
if only because I almost died there once

Even now
   I face the desert
with the coppery taste of dread in my mouth

The years that have passed
   only sharpened the winds
  the sun burns brighter off the rocks
  the sand still plucks at my feet
   quietly trying to drag me down

It is not home
  to be here
 for I know no such haven
but it is a familiar place
  that I have returned to

The first time I came here
 the sirocco brought me
   lethal vengeful driving winds
  chasing me across the sand
until I found refuge at a lost and forgotten oasis

When the howling winds passed
 I finally found a respite
  in the quiet
from the insanity
 I had left 'cross water and dunes

I might have stayed there forever
  safe behind walls and wastes
  had she not appeared at the gates

   tired, sad and lonely
like I remembered being

We shared those walls
  only for a moment
before the flames consumed us both
and I returned to the sands
   broken and reborn

Years later
  I stand on the wall again
looking back
  over my disappearing road

Waiting
   for I know she will return
 as I did
but this time
   I have mastered the flames
that once destroyed me

Chapter 7: The Sands

Around the fire
   a ring of chanting faces
voices crying out
   carrying into the darkness

Ghosts I buried within these walls
   before returning to the world
at sunset they rise again
   to haunt me 'til dawn
Lost angels
  like vultures
   gathered at my shoulders

A ring of maidens
  cries shrill and sharp
A ring of soldiers
  voices gruff and low
Together they sing a harmony
   filled with all the pain and treachery
   of the world beyond the dunes

The ghosts are from my memory
  both sharper and weaker
   than corporeal foes
But they know my weaknesses
  chanting them in dreams
gifting me with nightmarish visions
   when I close my eyes
  sleep tortured and sweaty

The sands are dead
   I killed them
  just to drive the world back
when insanity washed about me
  like the rising tide

No friends, no faith, no survivors
  just havoc and devastation
    in a quest for peace
I nearly killed a world to have it

I tried once
  to bury my memories here
    as my winds had buried the stone
  but time and storm uncovered both
Reminding me
    that I fell in love at this oasis
  and fled in failure and disgrace

Returned
  I find a kind of victory
the kind a sandstorm knows
  in destroying a mountain

I built the citadel
  invincible as my dreams
    as strong as my love
    as endless as my memory
it survived when I left
  survived until I returned

A ring of ghosts
    about my fire
    about my heart
The lost oasis
    protected by sands, storm, stone, and legend

And so I close the link
      begun by that first terrible storm
Tomorrow's altar is a forge
  crafting a chain in fire and blood
Hammerstrokes ringing
  across the silent desert
the fading echo
  of the Guardian's song

Dawnsquest

Chapter 1: Seeker

In all the years of wandering
  I don't suppose
    that I ever wondered
  what might lie beyond the desert

When I first found the sands
  I was running for my life
    and I only survived
  when fools feared to follow

I made it farther than any wanderer ever had
  but I stopped at the oasis
    and then fled the fortress
back to the border sands

Today I have walked here
  pausing to remember my road
    and to pay homage to my ghosts
  but I am not here to heal

It is finally time to transcend the desert
  the dawnsquest only begins
    at the Citadel
  and looks across the next wall of ridges

Once I walked
    where fools feared to tread
  now I must
    where even angels dare not go
  and find Seeker's path

Chapter 2: Horizons

As the sun comes up
I can see the world again
  an almost endless sea of dunes

To the west
  there is a dark line
    a ragged wall of bladesharp granite
    made soft by distance
Beyond that wall
  there is a world I remember
  a false green sterility
    filled with hollow fools
     and empty silence

About me
  I can smell the oasis
    shade and sweet water
    protected by the stormfury
    and the ghost of the last Guardian

I could stay here forever
  bringing his song alive again
  content and safe
    within the power of these walls
but night has ended

As the darkness flees
  I am strong enough to look east
It is from there
  that the silverfire comes
a line of argent
  stretching outward like a crack
  splitting earth and sky

About me, in the dawn
  the Citadel is reborn

   whole and mighty
    in the first moments of sunlight
    for the moments that I remain

I stare blind into the sun
  knowing the dawnsquest
    is a path that runs beyond the sand
going beyond this fortress
    like the fortress went beyond the wall
    and the wall went beyond the world

Chapter 3: Eclipse

They never told me I'd love you both
or that I could have neither
When I walked away
I left so much behind
that I'll never see again
never know again
and I might grow old
before I touch you again

The darkness was a cold kiss
in the brightness of noon
but the medicine man foretold no eclipse

The half-night instead drew me a path
running down across the valley
and then into the wilds beyond

Chapter 4: Crossroads

I wonder if there is a place
  where old lovers
    long lost
    can meet again

In my mind I see such a haven
  a room lit by eight dim candles
    cedar walls with no eyes
      no memory
  a warm down comforter
    over a soft deep bed
    for two lovers to touch
      to remember

I can imagine you next to me
  purring quietly as you sleep
    curled up against the slight chill
    as the candles burn low
  one eye slowly opens
    as I run a hand down your side
    an old familiar smile

I wonder if there is a crossroads
  where old lovers
    like us
    can meet again

Chapter 5: Walker

Each face
   it seems
  that walks into my life
 walks out again
  without even a goodbye
like clouds passing overhead
 gone so quickly
  regardless of my words

I find the road
  a lonely cruel master
  as each step is a task
  and each dawn a triumph

Behind me
  a row of milestones
stretching back
 past haze and horizon
Before me
  a span of wilderness
running on
 past my farthest dreams

I'd leave a crossroads
  for us to meet
if there was someplace
  more elaborate
   than a single trail of footprints
 for me to leave word

I can
  at best
 carve a memory
  into a stonepost monolith
 as a goodbye
where it might be found

I might
   at least
  leave a marker
as tomorrow
  is still too late
but better than never

I will
   at last
  find the road
   that I originally sought
and see your face
  in a cloud
as I walk

Chapter 6: Rainbow

In the morning there will be a rainbow
 to remind me that it rained all night
Cold
  but it's a comforting sound
  lying here alone

They tell me time is the magical element
    in making the world better
   but watching vines climb a mountain
   hasn't helped me forget her

If the sky stopped crying
  I might not be reminded
but it rains even here in the desert
  her face in every drop that falls
    every rip of thunder
    every dawn rainbow

They tell me that's the price
    for falling in love
   even with a stranger
never being able to forget her
there is suddenly a world of things out there
   that bring her to mind
a song, a flower, even the sound of thunder

Lying alone in the darkness
  her face hovers before me
    a kiss just out of reach
but to sleep only makes it worse
  because I dream of happier times
    happier endings

As dawn breaks the storm ends
  a world of grays
    blurred by the mist

the only color is the rainbow
  stretching over me like Bifrost
  promising a pot of gold
    to whatever fools and lovers
   might be awake at this hour

I might imagine
  that the rainbow marked the horizon
  showing where to find her
    like following the Northstar
but what fool ever found the leprechaun's gold?

Like my dreams and the thunder
  it is all fool's gold here
gone before I take three steps
  without a trace   without a sound

It rained all night
  a horde of invisible mice
    stampeding across my roof
  gone when I turned to look
   like that happy dream
    when I reach out to grasp it
   or the fool's gold
    when I search the horizon

Chapter 7: Stone Orchard

Sunrise strikes like a blow
   forcing me a step backward
  until I regain my road
Walking into the sands

I still feel safe here
  in the shadow of the last Guardian's ghost
In my heart he still echoes
  but I'll never hear that song again

Before me
   on the dawnsquest
  the first glimpse at tomorrow
  the last look at my oasis

Giant black walls
   harsh in the first light
I am reminded of a tombstone
   dominating that valley
it is fitting

So many dreams died there
  mine and those of other fools
that if the desert allowed such monuments
  the sands would become a stone orchard
Perhaps the walls are built on headstones
  piled up beneath the ocean of sand
It has swallowed enough people
  kings and other fools
and never once rippled

As I will remember it
  it can be the marker
   for all the travelers who passed
  we have left no other sign here
Only the Citadel survived

   weathered stone eternal and invincible
It takes a special heart
  to hear the fallens' songs
     deathsongs others might mistake for wind
but at dawn it is still
  and the walls still sing to me

Chapter 8: Impossible

There is an unbroken horizon before me
  a beckoning call
    rising with the sun

A bitter heart drives me outward
  thru rain and dark despair
a melancholy silence
  still and empty

Do you ever call my name
  jumping up
    from the edge of a dream?
I would like to think so
I would have liked to stay
  but I suppose
that was an impossible task
  just like loving you
    turned out to be

This world that lies before me
  is an impossibly large place
I could hide out there forever
    beyond the world
    beyond the noise
it would be easy
  to make coming back impossible
my memory is the only map
  of where I have ever been

Chapter 9: Fool's Quest

I'm waiting for the knock
   that will never come
The one that tells me
  I have to be alone
    no more

I have tried and failed
  to create that sound
  to end the isolation
But I have become larger than life
   where the image leaves no room to live in

No woman will cross that barrier
  to stand before the world unafraid
They have created me a monster out of a man
  and condemn me for it

I lie there in the darkness
   listening to the sounds of the night
   waiting for a sign
a ringing phone   a ringing doorbell
   sometimes even a smiling face
the smiles are fake
   the smiles are faked
but the silence is real

Sometimes
  the only sound that keeps me sane
  is my crunching footsteps
    receding from the light
     knowing there will be no answer

It is a damnation
  any woman could rescue me from
  even one night would give me hope

I remember being a monster and a hermit
  born alone
  living alone
  probably dying alone
    because no one would give me a chance

The dawn of hope is a lie
the sunrise is the dawn of fate
  a dawnsquest to lose everything
    for a gamble on what might be found
  beyond today

Alone
  on my foolsquest
    for a rainbow

Starfall

Chapter 1: Tears

Years ago I walked
　into the morning rain
without a chance to look back

I'd have seen you standing there
　cold and shivering
falling water mixed with falling tears

Now I hold that memory
　close to my heart
as I could not hold you then
as I cannot touch you now

I have become a ghost
　walking through the shadows
of the world I once knew
　without casting one of my own

Looking into faces that cannot see me
  except in tortured memory
of times long past
  battles long forgotten
    passion long gone

If I were flesh before you now
would you cry in terror
  or happiness?

I tried to love you once
  in the face of the hurricane winds
but the stormfury bound me
and I had only the choice to die or walk away

I might have died
  from the way I am remembered there
and the relief shown at my passage

Can the bridge
  once burned
ever be rebuilt?

Or was I forced to damn us all
  by walking into a wall of falling tears
when I could not have you
  could not hold you?

Chapter 2: Darksong Rising

There is a song in the winds
  calling out to me
    through the lonely night
Foolish
  I followed it outward
    on a path so long that even it has forgotten
      being the yellow brick road

There is a song in the wilds
  calling out to me
    through the bitter night
One stride forward
  to wake from the walking dream of sapphires
    and sand dunes that a moment ago
      were waves

There is a song I hear
  whispering my name
    like wind in the darkness
A step
  bridging a chasm
    so wide that eternity hides
      at its bottom

There is a sadness I remember
  echoing in my voice
    like thunder rolling around me
A road
  in the vision I see
    but still wilderness in the steps I take
      a song calling to me

Chapter 3: *Angel*

I had a dream about an angel
  flying in the sky above me
wreathed in a nimbus of moonlight
  like St. Elmo's fire

Her eyes smiled at me
  from a mountaintop ahead
singing a calling song
  crystal through the cool night

I got there to find her gone
  just the echo of her laughter
and the memory of her smile
  as the mist began to fall

Like St. Elmo's Fire
  the mist embraces me
a cool midnight kiss
  in a world lit by stars and moons

Inside me the dream still lingers
  survivor of the falling
  survivor of the failing
a memory of other days
  the eyes and laughter of an angel

Chapter 4: Stormfury

Somewhere in the downfall
  I hear a voice cry out
a scream like metal shearing
  unmuffled by the storm

It brings me back from a daydream
  slogging through the mud
encased in the muck and mist
  and surrounded by the night

Somewhere out there
  is a moon obscured
and stars to both horizons
  behind the wall above me

Lightning paints my path
  through twisted canyons and angry ravines
Thunder an ugly growl at my shoulder
  rolling over me like a flood
In the running fury of the storm

Chapter 5: Warrior

Even here
  I hear the horn
    calling thru the storm
    drowning the crashing thunder
    shattering the downfall

Somewhere over the horizon
  they remember the Wars
the time of madness is a vivid memory
  but the horn rings
One fool who would summon

Steps behind me the devastation lingers
  even the sky is darker
with the fallen stars
  and howling darkness

The only light to be had
  is a fire slowly consuming me
  shining from my eyes
like some ancient dragon
  woken from his slumber
    by the crystal-pure note
or perhaps it is the rebirth
  of the warrior
the Red Lance

Chapter 6: Starfall

Once upon a time
　I had a road
In the heavens
　a path of stars lit the way
But darkness arches over me now
　where the stars fell

Howling stormwinds embrace me
　rain cascades down
the world comes down to a few feet of mud
　and the bitter northern winds

On the forward horizon a new star appears
　pulsing with fate and promise
Lancing through the clouds
　as though riding the call of a horn

It rivets me for a moment
　in release the dice are cast
　in prayer the bridges burn
I stand
　alone
on the far edge of darkness
　beyond the insanity
My eyes see one star
　　where my heart remembers a field of diamonds
one road
　　where I once saw thousands
one fate
　　where I once walked free

Chapter 7: Crimson Dreams

I had a dream that the world was afire
  columns of black smoke
    like pillars upholding the sky
acidic steaming rain poured down
  coating the scene with a flavor of madness
Gunfire
 —tongues of ravening flame
    roaring out of windows and alleys
screaming death strewn like mushroom spores

By dawnsglow
  a saner world emerges from the echo of the dream
a dream so rich that the two bleed together
  mixing fact and fantasy
so close they become nearly one

I remember the city burning in my mind
  I was the sole survivor of the Wars
blood running in the street
  smoke hanging like a fog over us
mad tide rising

There were lifetimes bled out
  out there fighting the chaos hordes
a final day for too many warriors
  The Red Lance emerged
perhaps one or two others escaped

The armor appeared before me today
  empty and beckoning
as before
Blaze and his sons are swallowed in the Becoming
  the least-son reclaiming me

I had hoped that the wars had ended
  but a new generation of fools has emerged

vain and arrogant
   looking to claim the world to their petty games
understanding only force

With a final wistful glance outward
   I seal my fate anew
destroyer on a justice path
   warrior reborn

Inside the Citadel of the Oasis
   a ghost sings quietly
   a song of memory and hope
      tinged with acid-drawn pain
About them the kralizec rages
   grinding mountains and fools down

Looking outward I feel the winds rise
   answered by a stirring in the depths of my soul
      like daemons emerging unchained
      to rend the world
Before me the servants of madness gather
   a host reaching the bloodied sunset
chants echo long and distorted in the gathering storm
The Master of Darkness laughs
   I can almost taste his taunts
      as his fools swarm up like a tide

Night arches over me
   dark broken only by a blood-red moonseye
      blood-red feral eyes
   blood-red spear
I dream crimson visions
   crimson fate

Chapter 8: Hellstorm

At night the Darksong haunts me
  memories and visions of madness
they engulf me
  under a sky of bloodred darkness

Strangers turn into lovers
  and back again
Comrades become foes
  and back
Midnight is morning
  and back

The cries I might hear
   or make
  are drowned in the roar of the Darksong
For a moment
   I stand in the eye of a hurricane
  while cries of the damned and doomed swirl about me
I can hear every soul in hell out there
  some of them know my name
and remember me from better times

With a step I plunge into the cacophony
  winds rip me
   the rain is a hammering blow
I am deaf and blind
The memory of yesterday's peace
  is a soft twinge of pain
   a fading sunset
    a lover lost over the horizon
   while the storm grinds the world down
do any others survive here
  in the hellstorm?

Chapter 9: Midnight Eyes

You stare into my eyes
  but cannot guess my thoughts
It is just as well
  for the hell in my mind
    is not for innocents

If I appear impassive
  it is because inside me there is a hurricane raging
    screaming to be let loose
  chained daemons howling in frustration

If you knew the dreams I see
  you would flee me in fear
like some murderous beast of the night
  I have looked through his eyes
    and seen the raging darkness

I would like to lie beside you tonight
  for a taste of your love
But in my dreams
  I see the wrath of madness descend
    cold steel fury in my nightmare

Perhaps another time
  when I finally force them down again
I can take your hand
  where the darkness is the night
    instead of my heart

Chapter 10: Cityburn

At the horizon a line of fire marks the city
  slowly dying in the night
howling like a maddened beast
  fouled in its own blood

Overhead the sky burns black
  a tangible darkness like an evil fog
One bloodred star pulses
  hanging like an overlord
fullmoon dawns eastern
  driving the animals mad in the city

The wind blows hot and reeking
  a foul stench originating somewhere near hell
and reaching out to touch me
  a caress like an evil slap

I stand facing the world
  alone on a ridge
  looking down as sickness flows like a tide
My cry of anguish
  swallowed up by the hatred
as I wade down in
  striking right and left as I go

I emerge
 gore-splattered
   on the far edge of the valley
Perhaps a step closer to my fate
  at least a step farther from my past

I sleep to hideous memories
  bubbling up from the cold swamp
    at the core of my mind

And when I awaken
  I lie in a pool of cold sweat
a darkness lit by one star
  moon glowing crimson as it rises

Chapter 11: Songs of Madness

Shroud my eyes in darkness
  where stars once shone
"Everybody," she told me
  "everybody falls out of love, eventually"

She fell
  and like an ebon chain
    drags me down in darkness
  like a watery grave
    reaching up to enfold me
  an icy midnight kiss
    hoarfrost rime on my chest
  as the river freezes

Nightmare tide around me
    madness rolling in over the rocks
  greenish evil fog swelling at the horizon
    traversing in towards me
There is a dead world there
    moonless and hanging
  starless night echoing
    cold and brittle madness

Dawnsquest (Continued)
Chapter 10: Sole Survivor

There came a moment
  brilliant with the promise of eternity
we stood poised on the edge of the world
  dancing on blade's edge with our sanity

One by one they fell
  done in by dreams
    or darkness
    or even failure
Cairns in the wilderness

One by one they fell
  until I stood alone
    surrounded by the corpse of the world
shattered by the quest
  as they were

One by one they fell
  no songs no memory
    just one walker
the last survivor
  of our dream to change the world

There came a moment
  bright with dawn
I stood poised on the far edge of darkness
  alone to my fate

Travels: The Winterstone Chronicles

the Winterstone Chronicles

Chapter 1: Song of the Lost

And in the fading autumn sunlight
  I gathered my brothers together
a glance back to the lands lost
  and then fore into the gathering gloom
there lay our destiny
  to claim those lands from the darkness
    those of us that survived

Come morning the company had dwindled
  somewhere behind us were homesteads
roads and cities springing up
  where our feet had trod
    and our brothers stopped

Desert-scarred we came
  riding out of the dawn into a new world
grim and silent save for the horses and tack
  rugged faces carved by storm and sun
    eyes both dead and blazing

Before us stretched an ocean to infinity
  mocking us with calm regard
I remembered the ancient Muslim call
  that we stop only because there exists no ford
    to cross that ocean
      as Allah must bear witness
but my army
  small in number and mighty in vision
would not be swayed by distance
  not after the desert

We built a boat
  and sent the horses back to nature
facing a new desert
  eternal in its emptiness
as dangerous as the stone behind

On the last cliff face
  overlooking the sea
    each of us carved a single line
  a memorial and a stone
for the day the sons of lost brothers came
at its base we lit a candle
  remaking the pact borne of fire
    a circle of grim angry faces
  brothers joined in purpose facing the darkness
and set out for our destiny

--*Song of the Lost*
Winterstone memorial, Land's End

Chapter 2: Farthest Shores

Will you shed a tear
  for all the things
    that might have been?

Yesterday
  we ran along the strand
    'neath the stars and gathering fog
looking for forever
  with the innocence of youth
    and the grandest dreams

When the winter came
  that beach became a kind of memorial
    where the ghosts of two children still run
Under the darkness of Starfall
  only ghosts can return there now
    to the shadow of the Winterstone

I remember that last sunset over the water
  thinking quiet thoughts as the light faded
about me my brothers gathered
  not once looking at the mountains behind us
    enjoying a last moment in this world
    before setting out for farthest shores

Combined together
  I could not guess
    how many faces and dreams
    we have left behind
     or leave behind now
    as the morning tide begins to run
  outward bound on the winds
Land's End fading

Together
  we will never see this place again

    never touch that stone
I wonder what our brothers will say
  when they tell their children the stories
    of the ones who continued the run

Together
  we will begin a new adventure
    somewhere beyond the tradewinds
secure with the memories
  the lovers remembered
    the lands crossed
      the dawns and sunsets
        the winterstone

Chapter 3: Fairhaven

I remember the sunrise
  over the spires of Fairhaven
 knowing I would soon leave
  likely never to return

It was winter then
 a time to give lie to a summer mirage
  and summer daydreams
 but we paused anyway
  a chance to say proper farewells
   as we turned ourselves outward bound

The spires of Greathall shone golden
  in the first morning light
 that is how I will remember it always
  looking back from the last ridge

Somewhere before us
 an ocean waited to be crossed
On farthest shores
 we would find our destiny
But today
 that place is only a dream

There came the moment
 brilliant with the promise of eternity
We stood poised
 for one lingering heartbeat

Behind us
 Fairhaven and the world
Before us
 Ocean to eternity

Here we passed
 outward bound

Chapter 4: Sapphire Dawn

When morning came
  the horizon was endless
    only a few clouds in the distance

I stood at the leeward rail
  watching the ship's shadow race the clouds
  listening to the wind in the rigging
It reminded me of the wind in the trees
  and a place far away now

We left it all behind
  somewhere beyond that dawn
    the security and promise of that land
  looking for a dream
    somewhere beyond the next mountain
  or now
    the next wave

You asked me once
  how I could just walk away
    but we only shared one language
The wind and rain also spoke to me
  telling me of other dreams
    warm enough to brave the cold for

Now it has me crossing the sea
  this dream
    too big for even a continent to hold
looking for peace
  finding adventure instead
    in the endless struggle to survive

This desert already has left scars
  touched us
    much like the sands after Fairhaven

It is there in the squinting eyes
   the set of working shoulders
   the gait on pitching decks
Voices used to forest hunting
  now crack calling above wind and waves
Hands calloused by sword and reins
  now callous from rope and harpoon
Hearts tempered by desert heat
  now face new worlds   old dangers

We survived the sands
  the great amber dream
We survived that last step on land
  at winterstone
    one last hope for the emerald dream
and now we survive the blue desert
  living on sapphire dreams
    haunted
  by the crimson dreams

Chapter 5: Nightfall

I watched the sun slowly set
  darkness chasing us both across the water
    wrapping the world in cold winds and fog

Today
  for just a moment
    the far-off clouds mimicked a mountain
  for just a moment
    the ocean was suddenly bounded
  for just a moment
while it lasted

When the winds broke it up
   we nearly cried with loss
  but continued forward
    still searching for those farthest shores

To turn back now
  without finding the other side
    ...might as well hole the hull
  and ride her down
as surrender

Each morning
   she leaps like a porpoise
  as we set the sails full
    running up to daytime speeds
      listening for the roar of distant surf

Each morning
   silence greets us
  another day farther from yesterday's dream
   eternity looming before us
  running before dream-filled visions
    as we do the wind

Standing on the foredeck
  bidding farewell to the sun again
I cannot remember
  how many times
    the sun has set on our quest

Too many years behind us
  too many warm places we could have stayed
    somewhere along that path
with no way to know
  if it might end tomorrow
    or continue outward forever

Around us
    stars and fog slowly gathering
    the world goes fuzzy along the edges
  as the full moon rises behind us
cool silver fire on the water
  the horizon ends
    just two hundred meters from the bow

Where we were alone with an eternity of blues
  she now runs through a sea of silver fire
    as though a chariot riding on the clouds
    dancing like magic across the sky
It reminds me of moonrise across the desert
  that same haunting silver beauty
    beckoning in the night

Chapter 6: Carthage

I speak of the time when the Wars ended
  but the fighting never ceased of peace
my foes instead broken and scattered
  while I carried on

In my soul the sounds of battle linger
  the elusive taste of fire and steel
    the roar of closing hosts
      as waves slamming into the cliffs
    scattering into a fine spray
and receding back out to sea

I stood at the van
  as the winterstone looking west
    plunged into a frothing sea of madness
      hideous gurgling shapes in the fog
        ridden down and sown with salt
      decayed corpses cluttering the valley
    green by the wan sunlight
daystar clothed in choking smoke

In the end
  the plain looked as Carthage must have
    ground into the salted soil
    and left to fester by triumphant legions
a land of beauty no more

I walked away through that land
  amidst fallen friend and fallen foe
    and those who were not sure
  there were cairns for the valiant
    and crows for the rest

In my memory
  the battle ended with a trumpet call
    ringing over the battlefield

both a memorial and a call to arms
as the warrior faced a new war

Today
  these many years later
    I understand the place I created
    sowing fertile fields with fire and salt
the desert that gave birth to the amber dream
  it began here

I am bounded by sapphire now
  sailing the blue desert in search of new lands
    as Odysseus returning
in place of the madness
  I have memories and guilt

There was a world there once
  filled with mothers and children
    laughter and happiness
  as Carthage must have been
or perhaps Troy

But I destroyed it
  a monument to my greed
    my anger
     my arrogance
      my hope
       it was a flawed paradise
    to be had there
     an empty stage filled with hollow men
  mouthing scripted lines to an empty hall
painting gray dreams on a gray canvas

In fire and blood I came
  willful and destructive
    a dangerous tool in unsure hands
I brought down three worlds
  as no man ever built with fire before

As Carthage or Troy
  only the ruins remained
    shattered by man and reclaimed by the desert
    and in that place even the survivors perished
all save one

There are none today
  to sing sad ballads of lost Carthage
    and none to sing of the Wars
 save that they happened
    and that a man came once
     and passed
      but did not pass again

Today none even remember that plain
  for I sing no other song of Carthage fallen
    or Carthage remembered
There is only the desert
  forgotten in its origin
    but monument enough for the place
  and for the man

Chapter 7: Hurricane

The storm
   when it caught us
  struck with the fury of the smith's hammer
   turning a horizontal wall of water vertical

Wind in the rigging screamed falsetto
 a howling ban sidhe loose on the deck
   greedy plucking fingers to drag us away
  the sails tore ragged in a heartbeat
   lost white flowers fluttering in a spring breeze

In the distance a lower roar
  leonine to the ban sidhe
   somewhere ahead like an ambushing beast
in the storm's midnight fury
   there was just enough time to grab for handholds
   and mutter a farewell to another past

* * *

From the beach
  we watched her come apart under the pounding
   wood and wastes strewn along the tide mark

Daylight brought storm's end
  calm quiet peace for our tattered hopes

Around us
   that place we had been seeking
  but the cost was yesterday
somewhere behind lay the winterstone
  on an unknown beach an ocean away

We are now the Lost
  that song was our destiny
On a foreign distant shore

  we might
    like Odysseus
  wander twenty years without finding home
Or we can begin again
  learning old lessons in new lands
    home now an impossible journey away

Until this moment
  I always hoped
    that the quest would come full circle
  returning me to that place
such hope is folly now
  unless the world is round and the journey straight

I remember the valley whence the nomad sprang
  these many lifetimes ago
Behind us the meadows of Fairhaven
  golden by dawn
The amber desert as well
  haunted and haunting
And now the blue desert
  impossible and unforgiving

Winterstone awaits us
   as do warm fires and loving women
  but the quest is not yet finished
another dawn into the sunset
  another world to conquer
    with chill in the air
      and fire in our hearts

the Blacksmith's Song

Chapter 1: The Catacombs

And so the dreams begin anew
  dank dark tunnels
    filled with brackish pools and green light
  cold ugly wind in the storm drains

I knew this place once
  another dream
    another time
  the night that almost never ended

Can you hear the screams echoing?
  they say people lived down here once
    before darkness claimed the sun
  mayhap they are other travelers
    lost to the surface world
a cold and bitter ghost lurks down here
  preying on the lost

In another age
  I fought the master of this place
    a war unlike this world has known
     hordes of ravening beasts
    glittering succubi
   dancing madness
darkness ascendant

That was the time of the Darksong
  rising from these tunnels
    where fell creatures hide
  like the engulfing gray nightfog
come to claim us

Have you never heard that call?
  ringing with ugly greed and callow madness
    his victims live forever in the dark places
  a cold hand on your neck as you pass

I was once his tool
  destroying a world for his pleasure
    and my own foul purpose
  I came with fire and fury
like apocalypse descending

It was a war unlike this world has ever known
  when I turned on him
    and wrought my justice there as well
  like the fires of the blacksmith
and the blows of the hammer

There was left a place
  some call it Carthage now
    but any name will do
  for only the ruins remain
and they tell no tales

There are only the tunnels below
  still festering with the darksong
    a cold ugly place
      where angels never tread

It is a war never-ending
  fought now in his domain
    with fire and salt
  blood and fury
and the angel's dream

Between us
  in the wan green light
    all his creatures stand
  quivering with the fear of our wrath

No laughter or prayers can touch him here
  safe in the folds of the darksong
    he smiles wicked and proud
  knowing he can be savaged here
but never truly defeated

That darkness can never be felled
  never quieted
    never quenched
  for it lurks in every heart
singing quietly

But I have not come on the path of righteousness
  no angel's dream guides me
    mine is the mission of vengeance
  I will be content to slay him without
because I can master him within

In a blink he knows to fear
  for he is immune to the white fire
    but no angel's hand has touched my blade
  it still glows red with the Blacksmith's Song
seeking a heart to quench the flames

My smile no less evil than his was
  just a second ago
around me those arrayed hordes quail
   clamoring to flee their trap reversed
     there are screams of terror and the Blacksmith's Song

It was a war unlike this world had ever known
   darksong waxing and waning across horizons
     content to corrupt those innocent souls
Until I learned the Blacksmith's Song
  his blade lighting the tunnels a terrible red glow
    swallowing the green light

There was a truce for a time
  but he broke it in his greed
    looking to visit me his wrath
Can you hear the screams from the tunnels?
  one of those lost souls was a seer once
the dragon awakened instead
  and now I bring vengeance to this place

The dreams begin anew
  dank dark tunnels
    filled with brackish pools and green light
  and that cold ugly wind in the storm drains

He has shown me the path
  and awakened the last Carthaginian
    those cries of madness give way to terror
  as my footsteps approach
for it will be a war unlike this world has ever known

Chapter 2: the City

In the cry of a nightbird
  I heard an echo of her voice
    it took me back to another age

We stood together
  arms entwined and hearts racing
    looking down from a balcony
  as the Festival crowds danced below
    somewhere in the stars and laughter and her eyes
      the magic was born

It was the birth of summer in the rites
  ripening fields of grain lined the roads
    orchards grew heavy and fat
  and our love blossomed as well

We had but a few summer months together
  before a shadow crossed her heart
    I felt the cold of death in her touch
      and heard mocking laughter from the night

Have you ever heard of the Wars?
  I sought out the master of darkness
    and found him already safe in my home
  laughing

In my last memory of the city
  seen from that ridge north of the river
    it was still burning in places
    looted clean in others
ground into the soil and salted as well

In fighting the minions of darkness
  I had become one myself
    wreathed in fire and the steelsong

   putting to torch and blade all I had known
    for the betrayal I had faced
 in the form of a brother

He escaped retribution
  and still hides in his master's shadow
    together beneath the ruins of that city

In the years since that day
  I have crossed worlds and dreams
first there was Mountain
  standing high and unpassable athwart my road
    grinding down all who might surrender to despair
     and surrendering
  to those who would sacrifice yesterday for tomorrow

later I was a revenant in the Desert
  beneath a killing hot sun
    surrounded by the sands
     watching them slowly claim my lost home
    while I healed a fractured heart and soul

and then there was Sea
  a blue desert and the mountain known as winterstone
    no less deadly than the past
     in crossing it I lost everything again
    shattered on an unknown beach

I heard her voice
  in the call of a nightbird
    she is still quietly crying

Chapter 3: Stonedancer Vision

For eight nights I had the dream
  calling my name from behind closed eyes
    tonight is no different

I saw a land of darkness to infinity
  lit by falling stars
    dying songs

Each light that fell was gone
  silver flashing to crimson
    and then nothing
  each day the darkness grew

I passed through this realm
  lost and alone
    where even angels fear to tread
  beyond both hope and despair

There the dream always ended
  but tonight it draws me deeper instead

At first the sound is without meaning
  then it becomes a distant mountain's heartbeat
    it might be an ancient engine
    such an image is in my memory

Closer now it grows
  leading me to a soft red glow
    a cave overlooking my unmarked road
  the ringing sound engulfs me
taking me down to the heart of a mountain

With no wind to blind me
  I suddenly realize
    how cold the night had become
      cutting through me

But here I can feel the mountain's heat
  leeching the cold from my bones
    with the red stone warmth

A thousand miles down I find a cathedral
  lit by the fireglow of the flowing lava
    the ringing sound deafens me
  but the origin is clear now

Legends speak of the Blacksmith
  living outside the angel's fire and the darksong
    answering to no power save his own

Here in the heart of a mountain
  I watch a sword take shape in his hands
    his anvil like an altar in this stonemight cathedral
    red steel singing under his hammer

For an eternity I stand there
  bound within the sound of the stonemight
    lines of power pulse in the stone
      answering his call

There was silence as sudden as death
  the song ended
    and hung echoing into this vast cathedral
  as he looked up at me

His eyes were silverfire aglow
  the magic that had brought me here drew me in further
    for a moment we joined

His heat flowed into my limbs
  rivers of power flowing from the stonemight
    and I saw the road

The vision ended as the song did
  I opened my eyes to darkness
    a void a deep as the darksong

Nine steps brought me to the anvil
  on it I found the sword
    waiting as if it were an altar instead

The metal was cold until I touched it
  and then a red steel glow began
    lighting the cavern a pale memory

I heard the Earthmother whisper the name stonedancer
  and I saw that road again
    bounded by mountains and lit red

Beyond the mountains there was desert
  beyond desert awaited ocean
    beyond water there were mountains again
it was the red road before me

Chapter 4: Earthmother

She came down from the wilderness
  seeking warriors for the apocalypse
    men to fight and die for her dream
her call brought me thus

In another age
  I might have remained a scholar
    but there was no ignoring her call

It was like that night
  so many years ago
    when the Blacksmith first came for me
riding from that same wilderness

In a dream I heard her voice
  a call whispered on the night breezes
    calling my name among many
  but each name I recognized
    each phase of my existence has brought a new name
she called them one by one

The final name was one I knew not
  until I heard her call

She brought me to this valley
  her stonemight cathedral in the wilderness
    standing alone in the first light of dawn
      Warrior

The names called to the morning
  rang like words of power off the trees
    answered by the beast of darkness

Though many times my war has known her cause
    this is the first
      when I have fought under her banner

but I have been the Blacksmith's sword for so long
  I no longer question my fate

It is enough that I fight the Master of Darkness
  cloaked in the red light of vengeance
    existing in the balance between angel's fire and darksong

The battle joined is like any other
  in a lifetime of war
    covering most of the world
      and all of eternity

Once I was of the Lost
  proud warriors gone beyond the edge of the world
    and nearly forgotten

In our youth and arrogance
  we fought to the heart of the darksong
    seeking to break his hold
      wielding the might of the angel's fire

One by one my brothers fell
  twisted by the dark one to his foul purpose
    through night we fought
      but only I stood unbroken
        when dawn crossed our ruins

I tried to return home
  only to find the darkness already resident
    so I burned that place to ruins as well
      and turned in despair back to the wilderness

In a red cathedral I found the answer
  in a vision of the Blacksmith
    slowly forging a sword of many names
      icons like totems down the blade
        and I was each of them

With his purpose fused into my soul
  I returned to the wilderness
    wandering as before
    but the Earthmother called
    seeking warriors for the apocalypse
   men to fight and die for her dream
calling my name in dream and midnight whisper

Chapter 5: Cathedral

My cathedral was the sky
  a symphony as grand as the wilderness
    ringing through the rocks and trees
      with the unquenchable fury of an avalanche

The mountains stood sentinel
  pulsing with the gathered power
    trees swayed and limbs snapped taut
      the first screams started in the canopy

Off in the distance I heard her song begin
  mysterious harmony
    and yet as familiar as my heartbeat
  a ringing counterpoint to the distant thunder

For another moment I felt it rise
  and then the song engulfed me
a baptism by song
  followed quickly by the driving rain

I have known torture less painful
  than the beauty of her song
    gathering me within its folds
      closer and closer to that whirling center

My cathedral had been the sky
  and the altar was now a towering anvil
    reaching from mountain to stars
      an eerie calm settling in its shadow

But for the grace of her song
  I would be lost now
    hammered down by that monster
  ground out like an ant

Even now I feel her caress
  a glowing nimbus of power
    coming between me and the storm
    as the song drags me forward

I remember daylight
  it was just failing when she found me
    the darkness is growing thick and cold
    but still her song rings

On the mountaintop a flash of silverfire
  like a lightning bolt held stable
    from within it her voice
    calling the storm to her

Can you hear the call of the stormsinger?
  Stormlady moon to the wayward sons
    lover and protector on the widepath
    calling me like a mighty war-horn

My cathedral was the sky
  a symphony as grand as the wilderness
    ringing through the rocks and trees
      with the unquenchable fury of an avalanche

Emerald

Chapter 1: Dark Angel

I remember the sound of horses
  riding down from the ridge
    in the early morning mist
it was like the Apocalypse come

We had fire in our eyes
  steel in our hearts
cloaks streaming back
  like the wings of hunting birds
Gray death in the morning fog

They were harsh faces
  deadly cold laughter
    ominous silence
the tools of a distant dark Lord

At our hands many dreams died
  shattered to pool like blood at our feet

Behind us a path of devastation
  to make Sherman weep with envy

It was purpose bound to power
  fire wedded to darkness
    anger loosed like a storm on the land
  dark vengeful angels
    singing songs of retribution
  grinding down cities
    like a glacier reclaiming mountains

I awoke from a nightmare
  to the sharp tang of smoke
  there were no words to encompass the damage
  no tears to quell the fires

Somewhere over the horizon
  fires are still burning
    where my companions range

Addicted to death
  they have become the demons they dreamed of
    humanity sold for power

I have known the hearts of demons
    and rejected the darkling
  at my feet that sword lay broken
a look of disbelief on his shattered face

That morning
  I stood at the foot of a mountain range
    surrounded by shattered dreams
    tainted by both good and evil
  bereft of patrons and companions
    years away from the dreams of youth
still angry and still lost
  but still human as well

That is where she found me
  a cool touch for my fevered brow
    emerald dream for my empty heart
    lance for my empty hand
She came for me in the morning sun
  able to forgive me
    reclaiming my soul from darker fates

When my demon-brothers returned
  blood again flowed
    the fires were hot and fierce
  and dreams were broken and scattered
while night covered it all

Come the morning
 I could see their faces
   stretched into inhuman masks
    eyes like rabid beasts

I remember the Dark Lord
  hiding from daylight
    sending his servants forth with fire
This morning I can hear him scream
  threatening me with his dark angels
    my laughter brings him up short

I was one of his dark angels
  and the rest lay dead at my feet
not even the tombs of Carthage remain
  for him to recruit more
I have broken the Darksong

It will be an Age before he returns
  the darkness withers to light's touch
    as a new dream dawns
     reclaiming a gray world green
    the only darkness is a taint
    in the heart of the Guardian

Chapter 2: Winter Dance

It is the time of darkness
  when the touch of the darksong is strongest
doubly so tonight
  with Samhain winds blowing

All of yesterday's children are free tonight
  demanding recognition from the living
    pounding hard on locked doors and shuttered windows
  cries of rage
    mixed with resident's cries of fear

Tonight the moon rose full
  silvering the land
    and granting a touch of substance to the dead

They surround me
  my ghosts
haunted eyes silently watching
  listening to the music of the night

There is wind crying off the rocks
    whistling in pools and eddies
trees snap back in the breeze
  nightbirds sing to one another as they hunt
far below is the staccato roar of the falls
    counterpointing the symphony of crickets and cicadas
even the pop and hiss of the fire is music here

Within it all I dance
  celebration of moonrise in my steps
    promise of tomorrow in the stars

For so long
  night has meant only darkness
    home of the darksong
I have been blind to its beauty

and numb to its touch
for fear of its power
  but tonight I dance
knowing that it is only darkness

Around me I feel the presence of my night-brothers
  mixing uneasily with my ghosts
    crows perched still as gargoyles
  true black in the silvernight
true black among the silver ghosts

Overhead the moon
  witch, lover, and mother on the quest
    watching over me every night
warm light in this Samhain feast
  in her silver fire I dance

This night I feel the forest breathe
  sense night's children
    watch the powerless ghosts wait
I am healed of my madness
  and beyond their touch

In the first hint of daylight
  I smell the first touch of winter
    reaching out to clean the world
    thick winter blankets
      to help the forest sleep

It will be white and quiet here soon
  the world will sleep and heal
    slow regeneration before spring returns

In my own soul
  I have known the winter dream
    a harsh blizzard knowing no limits
    no remorse
    walls behind which magic may occur

  hidden from prying eyes
as the winter storm covers the world

On a mountaintop I dance
  surrounded by yesterday's ghosts
    wrapped up in a cloak of Samhain winds
It is a celebration of winter
  the birth of the emerald hope
    the beginning of the emerald dream

Chapter 3: Storyteller

I would tell a tale
  of the worlds I have known
but there are not words to describe it all
  for this world is emerald with spring
    and none of its children
      save I
      are old enough to remember fall

Would you still hear those tales?
   visions of endless deserts
    storm-tossed deadly seas
      sky-touching mountains
would you Know the smell of a burning city
  or Relive the cry of a rabid beast
    child of a world with no darkness?

I have known darkness
  fought it
    fallen to it
      mastered it
    and spent an Age as a warrior for each side

Would you hear the tales of betrayal?
  of lovers lost for greed of a coin
    or brothers seduced by corruption
would you care to Know Evil?

Then gather at my knees
  and hear my words
for that is my purpose
  to remember darkness for this world

It will come in time
  have you no doubts
    for I could only defeat it
it cannot be destroyed

only banished
and someday one of you
  my children
    will be borne to corruption
    will fall to the seductive promise
will release the Master of Darkness

When that day comes
  I will raise a mighty host
    and battle will again be joined
      destroying this world in its wake

" ...?"

No, my daughter
  I will not slay that child
    liberty is a choice
      and darkness the risk
The Guardian may not interfere
  for one of the Darksong's children will return
    while the rest will fall

" ...?"

Because I was a child of the Darksong once
  possessed by darkness
In rejecting his dream
  I gained the power to defeat it

Even now I hear that song
  wailing faintly in my heart
It is that distant Dark Lord
  howling in frustration
    that he may not touch this world
  the only darkness it knows
is broken within me

So I will tell you terrible tales
  children of this emerald world
so that you may take up arms to defend the dream
  even after the world fails

But I will sing you other songs
  for beyond the angel's fire and the darksong
there is the Earthmother
  this world is her dream
there is also the Blacksmith
  whose songs forged the way

This is a world of beauty
  but it yet lacks passion
    for this is the innocence of spring
    and not the fires of summer

That is my purpose in this world
  to remember
    and to teach you many songs
    that the lessons and memories of Carthage be remembered
for I am the last Carthaginian

I survived a war
  where even a world perished
    brought down in fire and blood
  because mine was the hand with torch and sword

I have destroyed armies
  burned cities to salted ruin
    ground down dreams to shattered fragments
There have been mighty lovers
  loyal comrades
    and dreams worthy of gods

Shall I tell you the tales of Carthage?
  perhaps the Oasis instead?
    or Fairhaven and Winterstone?

I remember dragons and trolls and princesses
  and wars fought for and against all three
There are sunsets to be known
  forests to smell
    chartless oceans waiting to be crossed
    and mountains to be conquered

It is spring in this world
  after the terrible winter
the emerald dream dawns
  but the passions of summer
    and the madness of fall
  still lie before you
So there is a Guardian
  who is Storyteller for this innocent world
One survivor of the War
  where even gods died

Chapter 4: To Remember a Chalice

The half-moon rose a brilliant red
  like a chalice filled with blood
but that is an image unknown in this world

It belongs in another time
  as I do
    but we are both here tonight
watching a memory slowly rise through the trees

I have not thought of her in many years
  nor seen her face since that fatal, fateful night
when we were young

I would offer the tale
  spun with the majesty that such an epic deserves
it was the mightiest of treacheries
  spun with subtle guile
but that is the past
  and not a thing I care to relive
not tonight

But in the distance still it rises
  a bloody chalice
    slowly turning white as the night proceeds
emerging like fire in the middle of darkness
  providing the only light to break that reign

I have known darkness
  slept in its cold embracing folds
    walked deserted beaches in the gathering fog
    and even watched the stars fall from the sky

At night I can remember the world that passed
  much better than the day
    because so much of my past lies in darkness
waiting to be sparked by the moon

I lie here alone
  on the far side of twilight
    contemplating a world with no use for my kind
  save a living legacy for future times
a sword in a place without war

I brood here
  at night
knowing tales to fill the night
  rapt faces in the firelight
    hearing my words
but not Knowing the place

I am the last of my kind
  the Carthaginian
survivor of a war that bathed a world in blood
    such that the half-moon might rise a bloody chalice

We came
  my brothers and I
    seeking to destroy the power of darkness
  each touched a different way
warriors in our own right

I came from a green land
  in ages past
A city by the sea
  standing proud and white
    content
  until darkness touched my world
in the shape of a chalice

She was a simple girl
  a tinker's daughter
headstrong and fiery
  but still a simple girl

The Master of Darkness seduced her
  each lie more subtle
    each step into yet deeper water
He laughed at me when I learned

There was a companion on that journey
  first seduced with visions of glory
    until he became a willing servant
 and led that simple girl astray

When I learned
  it was already too late
    all I had hoped for was gone
  and that simple girl with it
broken and recast with fire and anger

Together they tried to break me
  knowing what despair would yield
    and together they nearly succeeded
  but I did not die quietly
and I took a world with me

Into that battle a simple boy was cast
  from it he emerged something else
    a daemon from the ancient legends
  tool of the darkling
destroyer of worlds

That ancient city overlooking the sea
  I burned it to the ground
    just to make a point of honor
  and deny them further victims
and yes, from anger as well

When I departed it was green no more
  only stone ruins and encroaching desert
    a wasteland of unknown origin
  haunted by a host of daemons
and the mighty storm winds

Somewhere in that wilderness I fled
  somewhere else I returned
    a forgotten ruined fortress called Citadel
  home of the Oasis

In it the anger passed
  as the ripping winds did

In time I came back to ruined Carthage
  still overlooking that sea
    but the ghosts proved to be too strong

I returned to the desert as its kin
  traversing those unknown wastelands once more
    going out into the heart of the darksong itself

I would tell you what lies beyond that place
  but there are no words adequate to the task
    only the haunting memory of stars falling
  casting a world into unbroken darkness
    casting a soul into unbelievable despair
  walking out to that delicate edge of sanity
and crossing it

The Master of Darkness almost won then
  trapping me in that place
    but he freed me of the memories and guilt instead
  and I returned
stronger than I ever imagined
  a quest emblazoned on my heart

It took me across that killing desert
  mountain ranges passed beneath my feet
    oceans yielded up unknown shores
      fighting me every step of the way
    but others were there to guide me as well
  a road through unknown worlds

Somewhere as I walked
  the world was cast in fire and destruction
    the dark one thinking victory finally in his grasp
dark angels unleashed devastation
  and laughed

When the Maiden came down
   from that green northern Wilderness
 I had not even dreams left me
  but she foresaw the Apocalypse rising
 and sought the warriors who would fight

We fought and died there
  all save one
the last Carthaginian survived
  the last dark angel redeemed
   the last of the company of Winterstone
my secrets now are known only to ghosts and Lords
  my memories for this generation

The half-moon rose a bloody chalice
  like the one that the Dark Lord used
to seal his bargains
  in a bygone Age

I saw many fools
  many friends
drink from that cup
  seeking whatever dreams might tempt a sold soul
but only darkness ever came of it
  and darkness fell to the emerald dream

Chapter 5: Vanir

In my mind I saw the War for Eternity
  it was no less real for being a dream

Fire swept the field
  lighting the sudden darkness that had fallen
Cold winds blew terrible
  bringing the fresh scent of death

One by one the mighty fell
  war chants ending in deathsongs
the greatest host known to legend
  they died there on that plain
consumed by fire or flood
  fighting to the last

On that morning a trumpet sounded
  calling my cousins to war
    on a mighty plain
      surrounded by terrible high peaks
Three armies poured in through the passes
  and not one warrior emerged

I heard that call
    and knew it to presage an Age of Darkness
  but I was not there
    watching those proud Lords battle
    or fighting by my cousins' sides
when darkness claimed the world

My cousins were of the Aesir
  proud warriors borne of a dark fate
to die to the man
  and to the tribe
slaying enemies the Vanir knew as well

They fought for passage to Asgard
  the right to stand that final day
a tribe of proud men and fierce women

Today it is spring
  winter buried them on that plain
a glacier came down and then retreated
  carrying them back to that frigid north
a land of valleys they loved so much

It was no less real for being a dream
  and it did not hurt one bit less to remember

They are the faces from my summers growing up
  brothers I went swimming with
  lasses looking to roll in the clover
fields and forests and meadows as I knew as a child
  consumed by flame
    smothered in flood
      wiped away by sheets of ice

I still wake up with tears
  to see the moon rising
  thin cold crescent like a blade
    waiting to plunge into the earth's heart
the sun will follow soon
  warming the brittle spring air
    made winter by darkness

Somewhere beyond the Battlefield a Hometown waits
  dimly remembered from before I began to roam
I suppose they think me dead now
  with all the cousins I loved so much
who could guess what might lie beyond?

From the mountains it was desert
  clear to the shore of that legendary endless sea
Eight Aesir and a cousin set out

one fine summer day
   to prove that monster finite
 by crossing her
but it was only one way

They may have returned
 or perhaps fell there instead
while I chased sunsets
 I simply woke up one morning alone

Summer gave way to fall as I walked
  the battles continued into the winter
fools and comrades
  fallen by my hand and my side

I find this spring world empty
   a sad and lonely place
  inhabited only by the children I teach and guard
The mighty Vanir warrior
  who still has nightmares about the end of the world
    wakes up with tears in his eyes
     and sad songs in his heart

Chapter 6: Starfall Memories

It was like the old days returned
  we gave vent to furies
    dancing to the rising stars

You might yet be too young to understand
  but there came a day when the stars fell
plunging the night into near-eternal darkness
  a domain where evil may rule

It began in my heart
  purged by fire
    and bereft of light and warmth
growing
  it encompassed my soul
    and with it claimed my world

By night
  ghosts and demons howled
    running loose in an unprepared world
  summoned in ignorance and anger
some call it Starfall

I watched some cities burn
  and cast torch to others
reveling in the destruction of a hollow empty stage
  dancing around the raging embers
    howling with those loosed beasts

Evil came near to claiming my soul
  with it He could have touched eternity
    just long enough to bring us all down

The War cost me my brother
  and my lover as well
neither buried but both lost

Ask me about peace
  but the War I was borne to yet rages
In the clouds the cities burn
  a thick black pall of devastation and sadness
darkening the sun
  and on bad days claiming all the stars

But all is not woe here
  even in darkness
    for I have raised up an emerald city
  where once a sea of desert prevailed
    for love of a woman who touched my soul

In the light of her moon I dance
  still giving vent to power and fury
    still beneath her stars

No demons spoil our celebration here
  in the springtime of our spring dream
but it is not a fire within our dance
  such would not do justice

Instead there is a ring of candles without
  eight
    for each cousin the quest cost me
within is a stone
  perhaps a cousin as well to that stone we placed
a lifetime ago
  on a distant shore
    in a world that passed
  and a day that shall never come again
at least not until fall reclaims our home

Perhaps then we shall again know lost angels
  and hostile ghosts
    and a cold world where true darkness falls

Outcomes: The War Of The Dragons

Dragonquest

Chapter 1: Dawn

I stand alone
  borne again to the darkness
facing the night with cold patience
  hostile eyes sweeping the night

Around me the sketch of a scene
  painted emerald
but fading now
   a lost and distant interlude

Are those your cries in the night
  watching me walk away into the dark?
Out there they may fight me
  but none can stand
    not now

I had a dream of a sleeping dragon
  coiled in his majesty
    ringing an Emerald city

Any who approached might awaken him
  but there were none left outside
and he was prison as well as guardian

Like spring he awakened
  one cold dawn with warmth stirring
two eyes opened
    surveying the false dawn glimmering
      before he cast his eyes outward

With a cry
  almost too painful to hear
    he leapt up and spread mighty wings
The silence of dawn was broken
  for just a few beats of departure

In the first light of dawn
  a moat surrounds my city
shaped like a mighty lizard's body
  with a head near the gate
    resting on a coil of tail
  but empty yet of water
and growing cold in the morning chill

I remember stories of a thousand wars
  fought across a hundred lands
    and a span of lifetimes

Though I have never been there
  I can still see the stone at Land's End
    and still taste the killing heat of a distant desert

At dawn the dragon of Carthage left
  flying off to wars unknown
    lands unseen
      and survivors of a holy war

Could I but see
  I think I'd find him
    perched atop the Winterstone
     keening in the morning wind
     for something that he lost
   when another world was old

This world is young
  and calls me in the morning winds
    now that no drake bestrides the gateway
  but he may yet return to his place
so I depart
  winds guide my eyes
    and stones mark my path

Chapter 2: the Journey

There came a morning
  brilliant with the promise of eternity
somewhere on the far side of yesterday
  when I promised to love you forever

That day still haunts me
  a ghost rising in moonlight
silver eyes piercing me with accusation
  all manner of hurts
    both real and imagined
  laying at my feet

Outside the wind rises
  rattling the window in its frame
    as though a ghost striving to gain entry
  held at bay by the candlelight

Inside I wait
  cocooned by warmth and light from the bitter cold
    safe from the ghosts without
  if not the nightmares within

A thousand nights
  and ten thousand miles divide us
stretching back
  like fence posts
    over the mountains

Even if I wanted to
  at this late date
    I could not return
  without a journey twice as difficult
    as brought me thus
It is still good-bye
  as it was that night
after a morning laden with eternity
  we found a separate destiny
    another road

Chapter 3: Wild Roses

Who might say just where it ended?
  I only remember waking one morning
    finding myself on the road
with only blurring recollections
  of how I got there

On my lapel a flower
  a relic of bygone times
dry and wilting
  as any good metaphor should be

About me other roses
  reaching out from cultivated rows
    thorns carefully hidden and blunted
  flowers properly bright
invitations clearly written
  but there is no mud here

After living so long in a greenhouse
  I find no dragon guarding my door
so I no longer must content myself
  with ordered rows and delicate rains

I have heard his tales of bygone times
  of dreams and loves
    of wars fit for gods
      and treachery fit for legends

His name was Storyteller
  and he was a guardian against evil without
    as he was a gardener for roses within
tending that little plot of land
  from a harsh and uncaring world

But I am his son
  in spirit if not in blood

and the horizons call me
  just as they called him so far from home

I knew no other place with my own eyes
  only with heart and memory
but I awoke to find him gone one morning
  just as he threatened to do

I know only the roses of home
  growing safe and secured behind high gray walls
    in an emerald city
but I have heard of other places where they grow
  wild and sharp
    in a land of predators and storms

On my lapel
  there is a wilting flower
    to remind me of home
but in the early morning sunshine
  I think I'll leave it in a ditch

It will not survive wild
  nor will it do me any good
    save to bring me reminders of a place I left
    one bright early morning
      with the summer sun blazing down on my shoulders
        when I set out
        looking for dragons and wild roses

Chapter 4: Chosen

I draw the cards slowly
  searching for my fate in their story
    wondering just how great a fool I have become

It is morning yet by the sun
  the rain has passed
    but the ground is still wet beneath me
summer is coming quickly
  but it is spring yet

It is easy to imagine
  as I sit here surrounded by trees and grass
    that I alone exist in this land
  one set of tracks to span a whole world

The faint breeze brings me the scent of distant roses
  lurking
    somewhere farther that I care to walk today
  stretched out in the shade of a single oak
alone and perhaps lonely

If I touched that dream
  would it flee my fingertips?
    running like the will-o-the-wisp before me
  as I sought to pursue
Or would it only lead me deeper into the swamp?
  by darkness and shadow trapping me
    when I have only just emerged from the night

The tale is in the cards
  but they speak of no great happy ending
    instead foretelling journeys and wheels
  surrounded by foes and lovers
    traps and destruction ere I pass
  I begin to wonder if madness was not a better state

Outcomes: The War of the Dragons

Then I was at least beset on all sides equally
  blade poised against the world's hatred
    armoured against the smell and thorns of roses

Today I have only my magic and skill
  small power to hurl against the darkness
guided by subtlety and shadows
    where I once bestrode the field like an armoured WarGod
      gore-spattered and fire-breathing across the field
  but the darkness that cannot find me
    may not hunt me easily
for in my heart I am still the dragon's son
  who is the last Carthaginian
    the last who remembers

Somewhere beyond the horizon
  I will find the place where the dragon went to rest
    when he finished his first task
for his fate is not yet done

With his heart I will fashion a new dream
  potent
    in ways that emeralds, fire, and darkness cannot be
With his blood and power to aid me
  I will bring a tattered dream low
    like a flag lost on a shattered pole
      atop a fire-plagued battlefield

I could not be left alone
  to seek a quieter fate of knowledge and peace
but who is to say which chose the other?
  It is enough to know that a choice was made
    a pact written in fire and blood
  coloured red over black
as the fire burning or blood still warm
  before it fades and darkens with age

That is the tale I find
  surrounded by dew-covered grass and wet trees
    assailed by roses from some distance
  and beset by the late morning sun

I have only my heart to guess where the trail leads
  but a dragon awaits me at the far end
    doomed, damned, and chosen
  as are we all

Chapter 5: Dreams

I know a dream
  borne of lines in the darkness
splitting the night like a falling star
  promising a distant morning

But to know that morning
  first is to know the dark
shadows lurking in every crevasse
  waiting and watching

I walk those shadows
  cloaked within their power
knowing it my own as well
  fire and blood and darkness

Would you cry for the loss
  never knowing the having?
would you mourn for the dead
  in a world without the living?

Can there be tears for the darkness
  that never knows the light?
can you sing a living song
  in the land of death?

I have known amber in my life
  emerald as well
sapphire dreams to follow
  crimson visions to flee

I have walked alone
  guarding mighty treasures
I have walked in silence
  dreaming sacred visions

I have known the dragon
  been the dragon
I have known the darkness
  been the darkness

I walk in shadow
  hiding from daylight dreams
possessed of power in fire and blood
  knowing a dawn that never comes

Chapter 6: Nightways

It seems so many years ago
  to stand unperiled
happier endings at my fingertips
  happier dreams awaiting my slumber
perhaps even happiness
  at least ignorance

Now I stand cloaked
  shrouded in haunting shadows
    defined only by a white hot fire
  burning in eyes and heart

Would you care to walk these shadows?
  tread footprints left on dark paths
    by the children of the night

I walk the nightways
  dancing by light of fire and steel
    surrounded by howling ghosts
      banished from light of day

Once I dreamed
  but it would only nightmare now
    were I to close my eyes
  for there in no peace here
I seek in folly

It is as dark as dragonsheart here
  by nightways hunting his spoor
angry, sad, lonely, fearful
  totem in the fire of his blood
    untamed, unquenched, unknown
  given over to forge the Lance
renewing a cycle older than the world
  making whole the sundered
    making stone the dream
      making flesh the love

I was born asunder
  lived through shattering
    rebuilt in the image of a furry newborne
I am the sword of many names
  forged in fire and blood
    two-edged power lurking sheathed in darkness
silver fire in the night

I quest the Dragon's Heart
  taken it will yield the power to build a dream
    unknown in this hollow world
unquenchable fury burning
  enough to forge the Lance
    I know dreams of Damocles
Shall my name be Vengeance?
  reaver borne and burning
    it is a seductive vision
      to lay waste the broken dream

I know dreams of the Howling Coyote
  dancing for the Buffalo
    holding a dragon's heart as the winds rise
About him the angry gather
  giving him blood to forge fire
    on his altar a world is broken
    in his dance a dream is borne
His name is Vengeance
  and he dances in fire

Dragon

Chapter 1: The Dragon's Fire

A dreamcatcher hangs in the window
  as I slowly come up the walk
    prayer and omen
    stirring up old memories

It has been almost a year now
  since I met the medicine woman
    and felt the fire of the eagle's touch

I was born anew that night
  forged in fire and blood
    of an old broken blade
  once sundered and left in the wilderness

It was an emerald dream
  filling the empty darkness
    dancing in a ring of fire
  as I once danced

in the ruins of a burning city
  after I set it to torch

As the crimson dream brought despair
  so emerald brought hope
    and sapphire brought peace

I was born a dragon
  nearly a decade ago
    and trapped within the scales of his dream
  alone and different
lost and lonely

Have you ever looked into the dragon's eyes
  and seen the anger waiting there?
I looked out through his dream
  and I remember every mile of devastation
    and every moment of betrayal

If you have never been a dragon
  you will never understand what it means
    to be hated and alone

I have been so long in his fire
  I no longer remember what I was like before
  so long ago
before that fire

Last summer the Earthmother came for me
  in the form of a medicine woman
Reading me in her magic
  every secret I have ever held
    every dream I have ever known

She could have judged me then
  destroyed me for my many crimes
    ground out that crimson dream
      and scattered its dust to the wind
but she held out her hand instead

All those years in the fire
  forged of me a nameless blade
unknown because no one ever bothered to look
  beyond the scales
    beyond the fire
      beyond the pain
        I was alone and nearly lost
until she held out her hand

She came down from the wilderness
  seeking warriors for the Apocalypse
    and found in me the destroyer of worlds

I remember once looking up
  into the fury of a summer storm
    to see her on a distant cliff
      bathed in silverfire and singing for the storm
before darkness obscured her again

She came down from the wilderness in such a storm
  shielding me with her song
    else the power would have crushed me

She sang for me an emerald song
  a smile such as I have never seen
    and showed me the way

I have been a year now
  unraveling the dragon's dream
    a trap linked to my soul
    binding me to darkness and fire

At the dawn I will take his heart
  binding his power to my purpose
    as I walk in the first sunlight in years

I have been nearly forever
  being forged and tempered by the fire and pain

   until what emerged
was the sword of many names
  each a history in the dragon's song
    a step on the dragon's path

And now the dawn where it ends
  beginning the emerald quest
    the emerald war
      the emerald dream

Chapter 2: Spring

It was an early spring morning
  when I first saw that dragon fly
    noble and graceful across mountains and valleys
  while I walked below

I wished that I could fly
  looking up at those glistening red scales
    free from the bonds of earth

It was an early spring morning
  when he landed and showed me the way
    but he demanded too great a price
      in my blood and magic

And then one spring morning
  they came and demanded my allegiance
    and offered me the option of death

It was
  so they thought
    the perfect trap for such a dangerous boy
  the safe way to bind me
freedom from fear at my potential havoc

They laughed at my folly
  and never dreamed I would become the dragon
None of us imagined what a world of darkness was
  on an early spring morning
    when I first knew a dragon

Chapter 3: Havoc

It was the voice of Apocalypse
  echoing down from the heights
    carrying on the winter wind
      filling the endless night

I heard her promise havoc
  as the winds began to rise
    a storm unlike the world has known
      anvil worthy of the Blacksmith's forge

Like an evil magic
  the moon engulfed the sun
    casting the morning world in darkness
      wreathing the night in fire

The medicine man smiled and capered
  reaching deep to touch my fortune
    he cursed me with his next breath
      and then fled wailing

For eight years the dragon slept fitfully
  content to ward my dreams
    until the sword of many names cleft the night
      showing my path like a comet

It was the voice of Apocalypse
  answered by a mournful howl
    dreams of other days
      songs of light and darkness

I held you for a moment once
  before it began
    before darkness and rain
      but I will hold you no more

Your curse as much as any brought me here
  beneath storm and dark
    an eerie calm quiet stretches
      waiting for the sound of horses

For eight years the dragon was my touch
  he fights me now
    trapped by darksong waning
      doomed by my hand

Will it be, I wonder
  enough blood to fill this valley?
    will filling it a second time
      be enough to atone?

Will you cry no more when it's over?
  know daylight no more
    for the storm rises
      and her song promised havoc

The Forestal

Chapter 1: The Forest

The spring rains erased the trail
  leaving me only memories of the way
    old familiar trees to guide me

In the canopy two ravens call
  shrill voices in the morning forest gloom
    sunlight in the meadows

The vision she gave promised darkness
  shattered time and again by light
    calling me here
  calling me home

There is a mountain in the broken distance
  I have never seen it in daylight
    but I will never forget it in storm

In the vales below
  I have known the wilderness
    beset by angry storms
  and plagued by visions of an angry dragon flying

The place has changed since I walked here
  and yet this forest is eternal
    silent and vast

It is not home
  I have none
    but no one will disturb me here
  just trees and ravens and broken darkness

Chapter 2: Tracks in the Wilderness

The sky cried all morning
  wiping away my tracks
    as though I never passed

There has been a world like that
  marred in my passing
    but cleansed by wind and rain
  only my memories of the change

We leave no path in the wilderness
 just ants in the face of the storm
    hiding and biding our time
      hunkered down until the winds pass
      and then the world is as though we never passed

In the morning
  scattered ashes from last night's fire
    rocks that show no marks
  trees old enough to be eternal
but no proof that I passed

Chapter 3: Summoning

The storm began in the west
  rising like all the hosts of heaven gathering
    until a mountain towered over me

In its path the trees bent forward
  as though listening for the coming rain
    unnatural silence as the animals fled before it

At first came a melody
  one voice joined by another
    until a vast symphony rang out
    about me the trees sang their greeting

In disbelief I watched the rain come next
  following that song with a dull rippling
    in the sky the thunder rolled forever
    sounding like a gathering avalanche
rushing down the sky at me

It hammered at me like a waterfall
  driving me nearly to my knees
    as some monstrous rite of purification
    until it passed over me
showing me the calm at its heart

Lightning-blind and thunder-numbed
  I beheld a man
    old and gnarled like his oaken staff
    wound into a web of song

He stood before me
  with the patience of a mountain
    gray eyes harboring eternity in their depths
    every line of millennia graven in his face

He had no smile for me
  standing there in his song
    and then he struck me with his staff

I staggered back
  falling to my knees this time
    before me fell the dragon's mask
    that I have worn nearly forever

I sensed within him a terrible rage
  echoed by the stands around me
    and realized too late that I was the intruder
destroyer bringing axe and fire to these trees

He raised that staff again
  and I could only bow my head
    crimes written and awaiting punishment
  but the blow fell before me
shattering the dragon's mask beyond repair

The staff touched my chest
  and time stopped
    as I was bound within his song

After eternity passed I found his smile
  cold and sharp like a herdsman
    all the weight of heaven rested on his shoulders
  but he smiled as he began his song

Within his tale lay all of history
  from the Great Trees
    to the cold
      to the coming of men
        the coming of devastation
I sat at his knee and listened
  bound within his song

Chapter 4: Judgment

As darkness fell
  I heard the cry of a nightbird
One owl screeching down from her perch
  Guarding the forest from the night

He stood before me
  possessed by a millennial anger
    such as only a Forest might contain

In a roaring flutter the owl descended
  exploding from the dark suddenly
    before lighting on the Guardian's shoulder
  four unblinking eyes reflected the moon at me
the Forestal's gray robes merged with gray plumage
  as though he stood before me with two heads

He spoke with a voice of thunder
  words of power to make even the trees shudder
    I felt a ripple of fear pass through me
      expecting to face the man's unleashed fury
    but from the dark I heard a familiar call

The raven had shadowed me for days
  since I first entered these woods
She landed on my shoulder
  opposite the gray owl
    creating a mirrored tableau
      before she turned to face me
        beak brushing nose

She called again
  deep in her throat
    one fierce squawk that silenced the entire forest
    and she smiled

I found the strength to face him
  as I once faced the might of the storm
    standing strong in the rage of his words
      answering with visions and dreams

Silence embraced the scene
  as Rembrandt might have recorded it
    images oddly mirrored but not opposed
      dreams renewing in the call of the Forest

For the first time perhaps in history
  the Forestal truly smiled
    the kind of warmth that makes flowers bloom in winter

He extended the staff in greeting
  touching my chest gently over my heart
    the owl voiced a friendly call
      before returning to her treetop perch
        but the raven remained on my shoulder

We walked through a forest suddenly calm
  embraced by a warm summer breeze
    watching stars as we walked
      in the distance the false dawn beckoned

Chapter 5: Transition

I saw the fire blaze in the Forestal's eyes
  and knew my idyll neared its end
    no more quiet teacher in the sunlit glades
      no more attentive student wandering the gloom

In some far distant desert land
  the darkness awoke from his slumber
    stretched out his hand and laughed
      about me the trees shivered in fear

We walked to the heart of the forest
  to a glade I had never seen
    save in tortured dreams

A jumbled pile of stones ringed the glen
  strewn about like some giant child's toys
    they looked to be older than this ancient forest
      old as the world itself

In the shadow of thousand-year-old oaks I stood
  seeing an altar blazed with handprints great and small
    some were not even human
      but each guardian had left his mark

I felt a chill touch in the breeze
  watching the Forestal set down his staff
    and then approach the altar
      at his touch the stone seemed to flow
        embracing his hand for an instant
      and then letting go

He approached me slowly
  the same forbidding glare in those gray eyes
    as the first time we met

Into my hands he placed the staff
  a branch from the mothertree of this forest
    preserved by her power down the generations
Into my hands he placed the forest
  domain of the Earthmother
    and then walked away into the gathering gloom

He set out for that distant desert land
  armed with faith and magic to battle the darkness
    knowing he was the last of the winter Forestals

I do not remember dozing in that glen
  but suddenly I was transported into another place
    to stand before the Earthmother

Her song, ever poignant, embraced me
  promising the storm's fury and the lover's touch
    it was the winter song I knew so well from older times
    but this time there was another verse

Above us the land slept as though winter-bound
  cold, dead, and wind-swept
    slumbering trees and slumbering creatures
      oblivious to her touch
    but her song promised spring

I saw a world awaken
  exploding with the fury of a spring-roused bear
    it was the beginning of a world
      and the end of one as well
        ripping across the land with the speed of sunrise

I saw the Dark One's Grand Dragon rouse
  the one who claimed me
    I quailed for an heartbeat
    but the staff held me firm

I saw the old Forestal laugh
  as the desert crags bloomed with spring and rain
    weakening the Wyrm's power in the wasteland
   I never knew he could laugh

I saw that monster blink in surprize
  and knew he could be beaten
   I laughed as well
    and awakened from the vision

It was morning and the forest sang quietly
  I gathered a mild rain about us
    and set out to greet those ancestor trees
     holding the dragon's fear in my heart
      and the promise of spring in the breeze

the Great Wyrm

Chapter 1: Memories

Midnight bitter northwinds blow
  bathing my soul in icy bonds
shackling my flesh in ancient memories
  lighting old fires anew

I have returned to a place
  long-since distant now
and players
  long ashes lost on that wind

Overhead the red stars glow
  feebly piercing the night
    highlighting a golden moon
  washing the leaves in a ruddy light

In a moment I will hear the rush of wind
  presaging the Great Wyrm
    arrowing through the cold night

basking in the evil glow
content with victory

Ten years ago now?
  I remember the night clearly
    but the distance is fuzzy with time
  only those golden eyes are clear
looking through me and laughing with delight

I remember a boy trapped
  one step between mountain and crevasse
    penned by snapping hounds on all sides
  knowing he would fall eventually
and be lost to the raging waters below
  no tears shed
    until a Great Wyrm came down
  in a blast of arctic winds
and a howl of dragonfear

He plucked me from that face
  carried me to some distant place
    far beyond the golden lands
  to some outer dark
littered with bones and weapons

I was born of fear and hatred
  rejected by light
    hunted nearly to death
      savaged almost beyond hope
        certainly beyond repair

Under a mountain I was born a second time
  nurtured by anger and vengeance
    taught by the Great Wyrm himself
    forged a sword of red fury

Unleashed
  I wrought in fire and steel

salting cities in blood
   shattering hosts under the banner of darkness
casting down the very stars for their light
   I was the damoclean blade

But somewhere within me
   hidden under the raging hate and madness
      hope still pulsed faintly

I might claim to have been trapped and seduced by darkness
   led astray and controlled by the Wyrm's power
      used as his unwilling tool
   but I would be lying
I was the destroyer

Darkness was the only hope I had left
   rage the only fuel
      anger the only strength
   vengeance the only goal

Like Surtur I came
   scribing my anger in black fire
      content to burn the world to ash
but within me
   hidden
      hope lingered

I knew of no way to escape the endless Night
   but I knew its strength
      and mastered it
within my hand the black flame dances
   bent to my will alone
      it was then that I challenged the lords of darkness

We fought by night
   as was our bent
mighty power flowing back and forth across the field
   shattering the land itself

one sword of justice
  one army of chaos
we clashed as only oceans might understand
  the mightiest fell to my blade
    the rest fed the land
  broken stone greedily drinking their blood

When it ended
  the dawn encompassed me
    for the first time in years

I remember simply falling to my knees
   watching a young maiden walking across the field
    within me the power was spent
  drained

In one hand a bloodied sword
  too heavy to lift
    even if I felt the desire
  about me the corpse of my army
burning at the touch of daylight

She walked up to me without the slightest fear
  balancing a spear in one hand
    one black raven perched on her shoulder
     red hair stirring in the morning breeze
    I looked into the face of Apocalypse
  and realized that I stood where a village once lay
at a place called Megeda
  there was nothing to do but bow my head

Somewhere within me
  I found a prayer
    knowing I would find scales in her other hand
  when I looked up
knowing I had found hope too late

She spoke a single word
  a name
    a prayer
    a reprieve
and placed within my hands the spear
  calling forth an emerald song

Chapter 2: Memories

In the first light of morning
  the memories pour back into an empty soul
filling the darkness
  as dawn filled the world

I am returned to that field
  scarred as though by wildfires
    perhaps it was
      considering the last time I trod there

I remember being born here
  bathed in fresh blood
    with a mighty war-sword
    upright in the first light
    planted before me
  like a crossed headstone
signaling the place

In that first light
  I saw a face
    a beautiful woman standing over me
  war-spear in one hand
raven on one shoulder

I heard a voice
  a name whispered on the first breeze
    promising me sunlight
  after an eternity of darkness
an eternity of hatred

I saw a Way
  scribed in the twist of a tree
    the fall of a leaf
      the rambling of a brook
        the touch of the wind

It was not a way of peace
  for there has never been peace in the world
    never a moment free from torment
     or hatred
       or fear
    but her song promised hope
    and that is enough to sustain me
  like a desert traveler
smelling a distant oasis

In that first light of day I was born again
  after an eternity of darkness

In my heart the anger still burns
  but I have mastered the black flame
I dance in darkness
  but her banner hangs in moonlight

I was born in battle
  but the War was old
    even as it approaches twilight

I have been a tool
  a sword of many names
    meting out justice
   and vengeance
and simple havoc

I was born cold wrought iron
  and I have lived through fire
    white heat burning and forging
   black flames twisting and forging
within me I have mastered both

Never having been forgiven
  I did not know forgiveness
    only rage and vengeance
  a black flame and a red sword
casting a world into oblivion for my pain

Outcomes: The War of the Dragons

She came down from the Mountain
  wrapped in song and power
    and forgave me
  a chance to redeem the evil I have done
a chance to defeat the darkness with its greatest tool
  for Twilight approaches
    when winter may be broken
  making way for spring

The world has slept for so long
  it has forgotten living
    rather than just dreaming
  but it stirs restlessly
and the lady walks the land
  seeking warriors for the apocalypse
    dreamers for the spring
      and storytellers to remember

Chapter 3: The Dragon's Wings

I sought out the darkness
  and found there was only one place
    where it could shelter me
  beneath the dragon's wings
but I did not need darkness that much

I sought out peace
  but found there was only one place
    where darkness was strong enough to grant it
  beneath the dragon's wings
but I was not strong enough

And then I passed into that place
  dark and warm
    perhaps even peaceful as well
  I have no measure of peace
never having known it

Beneath those wings
  I found that there was darkness to hide in
    enough to shelter me
  when the world would no longer wait
no longer withdraw

No other will know
  what it is like
    to be a dragon
  without touching that darkness
beneath the dragon's wings

Even now
  it is impossible to emerge
    to walk cloaked in daylight again
  without confronting the pain and hatred
that first drove me to ground

Within his shadows I mastered darkness
  became one of his tools
    Wyrm is a name on the blade
  but I mastered darkness
and became silverdragon

I glow like the moon
  lit by the silverfires of darkness
    protected from the daylight world
  lost and found in another place
beneath the dragon's wings

If you would seek me
  then your path will carry you to that darkness
    contained by scales and fire
  to the shadows to be found
beneath the dragon's wings

Chapter 4: Megeda

We gathered at the ruins of Megeda
  newly-wakened dragons
    as though worshipping at some ancient shrine
  perhaps it was
or will yet be

In another Age we will gather thus
  as we have in times before
    knowing the place
  that once
was the center of the world
  and will be it's ending as well

This is the time of truce
  old rivalries buried for the ceremony
    ancient hatreds left at the outer ring

Only the dragons are immortal
  we have outlived several generations of gods
    witnessed the end of the world at least twice so far
    overflown great cities and salted rubble
      hidden beneath glaciers' footprints

As each Age dawns we gather
  oldest of foes
    and bitterest of enemies
    we gather

In the stories we tell
  we preserve an unbroken line
    remembering each who passed
    and teaching each who has joined

It is said
  that at the First Gathering
    wings and bodies covered the land to the horizons

Outcomes: The War of the Dragons

I find it hard to believe today
  as the assembly barely fills the inner ring
    in each Age we dwindle
      as fewer are borne to survive the initiation

It is said
  that the Last Gathering will occur
    when only two warriors are left
      to carry on the ceremony of memory

It will presage the Last Age of Mankind
  and only one scarred Wyrm will live
    to witness the twilight
      before finally sleeping

Over the Ages
  we have witnessed many Last Battles
    watched the world die
     and be reborn
       cast in light and darkness
     fire and flood
     storm and madness

We have dutifully remembered each passing
   committing the best words to tradition
    and the mightiest warriors to song
   and in each Age
fewer are born for the many who pass

But in all that time
  no battle has ever been fought here
    none would dare break that tradition

It is foretold
  that two Wyrms will finally gather here
    the last warriors
      in a battle as old as mankind itself

Neither will emerge from the ring
  for their battle will be final
    a Twilight for the Dragons themselves

A victor will be crowned
  possessed of the traditions of eternity
    and he will sleep through the Shattering

On the far side of darkness
  another Age into the future
    he will awaken
     to a world that knows no magic
    and no dragons
  where even the Forest has been destroyed
and mankind is alone

Alone of all the creatures this world knows
  the dragon will remember
    as he awakens from his slumber
    so will the world itself
    but the unicorns of this place
  have no recollection of the old pacts
and no memory of the beginning

The elves will be so in name only
  without the heritage that had been handed down
    across lifetimes measured in centuries

And there will be only the one dragon
  still remembered from the Last War
    but hated and feared by the men he has found
  alone in their darkness
as magic is reborn

Chapter 5: Aurora

I heard the cry signaling Dawn
  given from the peak
    in bugling triumph

It rang across the valley like thunder
  waking the sleepers
    turning all heads to the east
      setting hearts to racing

About us the Night declined
  fading into the west like a receding tide
    slowly giving ground
      as though fighting for every inch

A single line of silver was to be seen
  shattering the darkness with promise
    dividing earth and sky
      building like an argent wildfire

From below
  we watched the Night pass

Tapestry

Chapter 1: Teachers

As I watched the sun slowly rising
  with darkness fleeing before its touch
    I paused to consider Aurora
      waxing and waning through my world

Long enough ago to be only legend now
  I remember a sunshine time
    smiles and laughter
      simple innocence and simpler fates

I remember one late summer storm
  how it climbed the heavens slowly
    rising like a mushroom from the ant's vantage
      and then curling over to soak me with its spores

Looking back at that day
  I remember how a path diverged
    or perhaps the road diverged from my path

I remember a first kiss
  and a last one in the same motion
    sealing me to the widepath
      casting me outward
        losing my soul

I remember in my mind
  the sound of the hunting hounds
    fresh on my trail
      baying with delight
      and hunger
  and menace
everyone thought me caught
  everyone but one

I remember fearing his eyes
  fleeing his laughter
    awaiting his jaws

But I also remember the sense of relief
  watching hunters and dogs dwindle with distance
    hatred and fear roiling in my heart
      enough anger to light the dim red darkness

They call him the evil one
  the Great Wyrm
    mightiest of the first

They feared him
  as the sheep might dread the wolf
    for none could stand against him
      but one of him own kind
      I know
  for I have seen them try

He took me to some nameless outer dark
  a place where the light shines but rarely
    an evil dim red
      where even the stars themselves have fallen victim

He began the task of training me there
  subject to fire
    madness
     hatred
      and betrayal
but I have known such ere then
  I grew up subject to such things

I suppose he saw the fire in me
  fueled by sullen anger
   and indomitable will
    a flat refusal to surrender
     even facing his wrath
whatever his reasons
 he began to mold me there

I fear it would have broken any other
  as it came near to breaking me
    several times
     but who ever asked the sword
      if he wished to be forged?

He wrought of me a nameless blade
  icons like runes down both sides
    bearer of silver fire

For a time I even led his armies
  seeking out those who might oppose his reach
    and breaking them
     not simply preventing them
      or controlling them
       but breaking them asunder
if you have never burned a city
 you will not understand his power

I have set many to torch myself
  laughing with delight and menace
    broken the finest knights and warriors

    cast down even the stars for their light
      brought about Night

I would have never imagined then
  that hope still lurked in the shadows of my soul
    having given up everything just to survive

But I suppose that hope underlay it all
  giving me the strength to survive the hunters
    or the dragon
    or the Darkness
I would not stop fighting
  and the world wearied first

In darkness the hope burned
  like coals in the nightfire
    I thought them completely cooled
      but I was wrong

They lit in me a prayer
  that I had committed enough evil
    wrought enough vengeance
    shattered enough dreams
    I sought to escape
  and in darkness
I fled

The Great Wyrm hunted me
  as the dogs had once
    but I had sat at his knee
      and learned magic and warfare from him
    second most powerful of all dragons
  bowing only the Master of Darkness
and his Grand Dragon

From the place of Starfall I came
  reclaimed sword held by another hand
    ready to do battle
It led me to a city he held

one armored WarGod against his own army
  in a crimson dream of madness
a legend known only as Cityburn

Walking from an eternity of night
 I beheld the dawn
   surrounded by the corpse of my old army
   and the last ragged remains of the wildfires

The legend has been told many times
  of that battle
   and others that followed
    of the riders that came
      the one who turned back to light
       the victory that broke the darkness
     it is all true
   I was there to verify it
   the first short step to salvation
  first step of another war
first battle of a Twilight

From that place I carried my Warbanner
  Crimson Sword sinister on field Sable
   almost to the ruins of Carthage
  the place where I was born
the city I first burned
  heart, soul, and birth of the Amber Desert

Atop the walls of the Citadel I placed it
  looking west
    towards that distant valley where the city once fell

I spent one night in that place
  where I had hidden so long ago
   in flight from the hunters
  long enough to say good-bye to many old ghosts
and hear the Guardian's song one final time

Chapter 2: Teachers

It dawned bright and cool over the Citadel
  as the sands again paved my path

I followed an unmarked road through the desert
  surrounded on all sides by wastes
    wandering from sand into headlands
    blinded by the cold winds of winter

My path has no map
  no road leads me astray
    no memory save my own could find my way back
    no home ever held me
      no hunter ever dared this side of the Citadel

In a nameless distant place
  fleeing from my first teacher
    I sought to hide among the hills
      no more WarGod astride the field

It was there that another claimed me
  hidden in a stonemight cathedral
    at the heart of a mountain
      lit by red light and rockpower

They call him the Blacksmith
  master of the red fires
    perhaps a consort to the Lady
    mayhaps only an ally
      possibly a foe as well

For years he haunted my dreams
  even as the dragon sought to deny him
    their influence waxed and waned
    like a pendulum moving slowly to rest

Time and again he did claim me
　forged a weapon of nameless power
　　warrior in black and red armour

In his cathedral I learned a song
　not the Angel's Fire
　　gleaming white and pure with righteousness
　nor the Darksong
　　corrupting mans' hearts and dreams to darkness

It was a red song
　outside the old war
　　beholden to neither Lady nor Master of Darkness

In the Fortress of Mind
　the Lady is immune to the Darksong
　　just as the Master of Darkness is safe from Angels
　　　hiding beneath the ruins of Carthage

But I am still a creature of free will
　subject to deception and argument
　　and able to forge my own path

With the Blacksmith's song as my blade
　I could challenge the minions of chaos
　　seek them out in the ruins of Carthage
　　　bring them down

Even the Master of Darkness was not immune
　trapped by his arrogance
　　he could not flee his trap reversed
　　　and suffered banishment by my blade
　　in a war unlike this world has ever seen
　and likely never will again

When I finished with his hordes
　I ground Carthage itself back into the soil
　　trapping him within his own darkness

only one army remained to fight me
  as had been foretold
    so long ago

Chapter 3: Dark Angels

On a distant plain
  near the inland sea
    I met the Champions of Darkness
     Dark Angels
    as I had been
  daemons in some quarters
unbeaten in any case

It was a place where the dragons will never fight
  a sacred site older than any memory save theirs
    but we were not dragons
     so we fought

Once they had been my brothers
  dark avenging angels
    tools of the Master of Darkness
     burning worlds at his command
       shattering dreams for his pleasure

Now they were my foes
  arrayed against me once again
    intent on claiming my heart
     entirely the daemons they dreamed of being

For one moment I wept
  trapped within an ancient memory
    of the battle that forged the first Redlance
    old comrades fighting to the death

Even the sun could not light the field
  so we met in darkness
    once all Champions within Darksong's touch
     now fighting to weigh its fate
       all of creation stopped to watch us War

The Battle of Carthage had been one of desperation
  salting a place I could not accept
    ending a flawed and failed dream
      killing everything before it overwhelmed me
I fled into the wasteland
  sheltered for a time within Citadel's peace

Cityburn was fought to force his hand
  sacrificing all the memories that survived the Amber Winds
    walking into his strongest bastion with a torch
      an incandescent invitation to dance
I left his valley for the mountain
  called by the Blacksmith to learn his song

The Return to Carthage was borne of anger
  misplaced and misused but still white hot
    reversing a trap with my song
      breaking Darksong's hold
I walked into sunrise
  child of desert heat

We met at Megeda
  sons of Darkness all
    under Darksong Eternal
      eleven blades

Darksong summoned black fire
  like acid spewing about the field
    vitriol burning trees, stone, and warrior alike

Steel rang on steel
  a symphony of unleashed anger
    drowning out the war-cries

Power and death raged as we danced
  ripping the very fabric of the Cosmos
    like one colossal earthquake

Each of us has learned from a dragon
  versed in both magic and war
    but they fought for greed and sadistic passion
    in my heart the fire burned

One by one I broke their power
  like old swords fought too hard
    until I stood alone on the field
    knee deep in blood and black fire

About me it dawned
  showing the battle ended
    sun, moon, and stars alight
      as I fell to my knees

That is how the Lady found me
  upright sword
    exhausted warrior
    broken darkness
      winter ascendant

Chapter 4: Emerald Dreamer

When the Twilight time began
  the world began to pass into darkness
    as Fall gives way to Winter

In the cycle of the seasons
   it is also possible to watch the passing of Ages
    and the turning of worlds themselves

In this war
  the fateful battle took place on Samhain
    the dying time of the old dream

When it ended the field lay bare
  scoured by the first winter winds
    leaving only skeletal trees and frozen brooks
     and corpses of the old dreamers

In my heart
  I always feared the appearance of the Lady
    coming down from the mountain wilderness

The old seers had told me once
  that such presaged the end of the world
    the dying off of the old dream
     the Winter-time

When she came for me
  I knew my time had ended as well
    leaving me only time to pray for a quick death
     rather than the pain I deserved
      as the reborn Emerald Dream arose

Instead she took my hand
  and led me back to the Amber wastes
    back to the heart of an ancient personal nightmare
    back to the Citadel

About us a world was slowly dying
  total chaos reigned and rained
    civilization itself sundered
     as though rent by cosmic fault lines
    perhaps it was
 such is the nature of endings

Within that place
  seated by the Oasis I knew so well
    she had gathered the seeds of the spring
    children who would build a new world

Son of a Dragon myself
  she tasked me to guard the keep
   as the Elders might brood over gold
    protecting it from the world without
   as all about us
 while we watched from the battlements
the world died

The time between worlds is a cold one
  enough to make winter seem tropical
dark enough as well
  to make night seem bright

I labored all Winter at three tasks
 at once Guardian again
   or perhaps still
    since I have always known the Citadel
  while also Architect
    rebuilding the old keep into the Emerald City
    something it has not been in Ages
  and Storyteller
   keeping the old knowledge alive
    and teaching these children the tales
     of both the world and the last Warrior in it
    to their innocent eyes
   even Spring was wild and dangerous
 but I have known Fall

Outcomes: The War of the Dragons

All winter I labored
  waiting for the Lady to return
    and Spring to release me
      so that I could find a place out there to live

One winter day
  I saw an icicle melting
    and smelled growing things in the air
      even in the desert wastes

I smiled as the sun finally rose
  glowing golden with promise
    something I have not seen in nearly eternity

She smiled at me from the Tower
  knowing my heart with her own
    and released me to seek my Mountain

I am the last Carthaginian
  the last son of the Dragons
    the last of the Vanir

I have lived in various guises from the beginning
  reborn time and again to Know battle

In the ending of winter
  another cycle ended for me as well
    but I had labored successfully
      nurturing a new generation of minds
      there were mystics and scholars
    wanderers and farmers
and one warrior to continue the line

She gave me twenty-seven days of peace in my valley
  something I have never known
    a gift beyond price
      even to someone such as myself
        who has watched gods die

As the moon arose new
  crossing paths with the sun for a moment
  my war finally ended
    but the Prophesy continued on
      and in his dream
    and my blood
   I continue as well
  teaching him what I can
guarding him still

Chapter 5: The Hunter

It was Spring
  and the second half of his fate was revealed
The Dragon of Carthage fled
  but he could not escape me

I had spent all winter hearing his tales
  until I knew them almost as well as he
    so I knew where to hunt him
     and how to bring him down
    it was the second half of his fate
  and the first portion of mine

I set out one fine bright morning
  with only a restless dream
    to hunt a dragon
     knowing what winter had taught
      and tired of hothouse roses

All winter he had told us his stories
  remembering a lost dream for a new generation
    a new host of merchants and scholars
     sailors and dreamers
      aye, and warriors as well

When the winter broke up
  and spring began to peek through the clouds
    he left us to find some lost dream he had
     no more the jailer of our emerald prison
    he was simply gone one morning
  with nothing but a cry of freedom
and a single look back

I set out that morning as well
  fearful that he would return and lock the door
    winter had been long enough
     I had no intention of spring here as well

Truth be told I was tired of the place
  so like a greenhouse filled with fragile roses
    it had begun to stifle my dreams
    but I could find freedom as I walked away

Out in the wilds I found a different breed of roses
  thorns no longer hidden
    vines no longer straight and true
      it was a harsher place to be had
        and I relished every step of the way

When the moon came full cycle I found him
  crouched in the ruins of a lost valley
    keening a song I had never heard
      for all the tales he had shared

Fire had lit the place once
  and floods had scoured it clean as well
    it was only just returning to life as I came
      it felt almost peaceful to me

But I had not come on a mission of peace
  and it was not our destiny to enjoy this moment
    he had come here to die
      secure in the knowledge of a task successful
        and I had come to kill him

He looked almost through me as I came into the clearing
  eyes that I knew so well from winter fires
    but there was a stranger in them now
      he looked at me with all the hurt of Ages at war
        and I began to understand what eternity meant

There was still winter in the air
  even as spring rains prepared to fall
    I came to him with fire in my heart
      holding a blade he had left me
        singing songs he himself had taught

I took his heart
  there in that valley
    I know now that the quest first began there
    so many lifetimes ago

I took his memories as well
  becoming the dragon of Carthage in some small way
    and all that had come before him as well
    thus the dream was passed
      as it always had been

Chapter 6: The Forest

I began this quest by departing the City of Emeralds
  seeking the gem
    at the heart of the dream

My road took me first to the valley
  that once was the birthplace of a dragon
    and as fate was told
      was his dyingplace as well

His heart was a ruby
  pulsing with slow angry fire
    a crimson and sable dream

But the journey only truly began with that ruby
  and it drove me further afield
    than I ever imagined a road could wander

I remember an inhospitable desert
  on the farthest shore
    of an unforgiving sea

It was the place I first found the wasteland
  around the Citadel
    at the place that I thought
      was the end of the world

Walking from City to Valley
  was like walking back in time
    remembering footsteps into the wilderness
    and the first champion to go astray

Astray I went as well
  lost and undaunted
    invincible within the tapestry of my magic
    weaving the threads of a dream

Somewhere along the nameless road
  the ruby led me to a giant forest
    quietly seething with ancient memories
    and bitter anger
    for I was Man
  my presence here was enough to awaken the place
and it's guardian as well

He has no name save Forestal
  and no function as well
    save Forestal

He is the Keeper of this place
  entrusted with old songs of power
    weaving power about this remnant
    of a forest that once spanned the world

I came to this place
  intruder to the dark woods
    and he struck me down
      shattering the ruby mask I wore

But when he judged me
  he found other dreams as well
    within me a dragon's legacy

I became a student again here
  sitting at the knee of this grim man
    learning tales forgotten before this world was born
    and songs no one
    save a Forestal
has ever sung

He took me in
  son of a winter dragon's dream
    and remade me
      until the day Spring reached the Forest

I had departed the City
  on the day the Winter dream was broken
    but the tide of Epochs flows slowly
  and many moons passed
before Spring took hold

The lessons simply stopped one day
  and we walked to an empty glade

There was an altar there
  covered with the handprints of every Forestal
    but the man who led me
    and he added his as I watched

Around it broken and fallen obelisks
  giving mute testimony
    to the passage of millennia

This place is the heart of the emerald dream
  a temple stood here once
    before the Forest was ever born
    so long ago lost

We transcended the place
  to stand before the Earthmother
    and there he left me
      for he was the last of the Winter Forestals
        I am the first of the Spring

In a dream I watched him enter the wasteland
  watched Spring rains flowing about him
    rousing the ire of the Dark One's Grand Dragon
    and weakening his power in that place

I also watched him laugh
  for the first time a smile I truly believed
    and knew the War could be won

I am become
 the first Spring Forestal

The Lady and the Dark One have returned
  awakened from their long sleep
   by the return of Spring

The dragons witnessed it as well
  an event we call Aurora
   when a world begins

At the Ceremony of Memory
  I smiled at the Grand Dragon
   so long the Lord of Winter
    and held the memory of his fear close to my heart

The old Forestal returned here afterwards
  joining the other hermits
   singing quietly to the ancestor trees
  We are Spring
and a world awaits our song

About the Author

Blaze has lived in many different places, including Kansas, The Ozarks, Breckenridge, and SoCal. He's also done a number of things, some of which are even past the statute of limitations now. The ones he'll tell you about (without the need for full anonymity) include being a bouncer at a cowboy bar outside a Marine base, a volunteer storm-spotter with the county fire department, and herding nerds at a small software company. He currently lives Seattle-ish and tells stories in most every form of English you can, and a few other languages.

About Knotted Road Press

Knotted Road Press fiction specializes in dynamic writing set in mysterious, exotic locations.

Knotted Road Press non-fiction publishes autobiographies, cookbooks, and how-to books with unique voices.

Knotted Road Press creates DRM-free ebooks as well as high-quality print books for readers around the world.

With authors in a variety of genres including literary, poetry, mystery, fantasy, and science fiction, Knotted Road Press has something for everyone.

Knotted Road Press
www.KnottedRoadPress.com